Grain Gastronomy

Grain Gastronomy

A Cook's
Guide to
Great
Grains
from
Couscous
to
Polenta

Janet Fletcher

Aris Books, Berkeley, California

Library of Congress Cataloging-in-Publication Data

```
Fletcher, Janet Kessel.
   Grain gastronomy.

   (Aris kitchen edition)
   Includes index.
   1. Cookery (Cereals)  I. Title.
TX808.F54  1988    641.6'31          88-14565
ISBN 0-943186-39-0
```

Kitchen Edition books are published
by **Aris Books**
1621 Fifth Street
Berkeley, CA 94710
(415) 527-5171

Series Editor: John Harris
Project Editor: Lee Mooney
Consulting Editor: S. Irene Virbila
Book Design: Lynne O'Neil
Cover Photo: Lisa Blevins
Food Stylist: Stevie Bass
Illustrations: Pamela Manley
Production and ✍ Type: Another Point, Inc.

Contents

Introduction   7

   Invitation to the Grains   7
   Eight Great Grains   8
   "Tell Me What You Eat"   9
   Grain Anatomy   10
   Processing Grains:
   How Groats Become Oats   10
   Grains for the Health of It   12
   Storing Grains   13
   Grain Cookery Tips   13
   Vary Liquids for Flavor   14
   About Sprouts   15

Arborio Rice   19

Barley   33

Couscous   43

Cracked Wheat   57

Hominy   67

Millet   81

Polenta   91

Wild Rice   103

Index   111

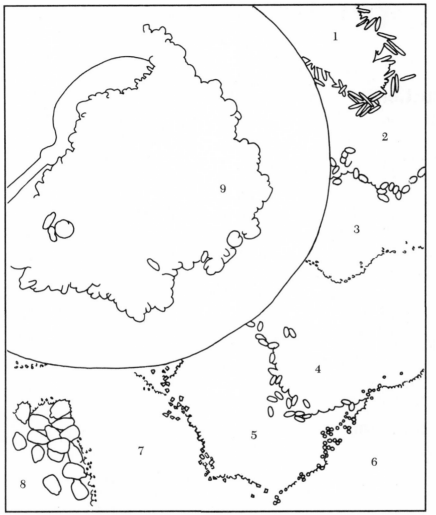

A Grain Guide:
Use this map to identify the grains that appear on the cover.

1. Wild Rice
2. Barley
3. Polenta
4. Arborio Rice
5. Cracked Wheat
6. Millet
7. Couscous
8. Hominy
9. Risotto with Peas and Pancetta

Introduction

Invitation to the Grains

For a Texas girl raised on steak-and-potatoes, the world of grains is constant lure and a constant discovery. I wasn't served grains as a child, except for rice and Malt O'Meal. In Dallas, where I grew up, grains were for horses. In fact, had Mom wanted to serve us whole grains—millet or whole oats, for example—she would have had to go to the local Feed 'n' Seed.

Today, thank goodness, the grain domain is rapidly spreading. Natural-food stores—even many supermarkets—are brimming with whole grains: whole wheat, oats, rye, barley, millet, bulgur, hominy, semolina, couscous, rice in different colors and shapes, triticale and more. And the more I learn about one, the better I want to know the others. The realm of grains holds endless pleasure for curious cooks.

For me, one good grain led to another, starting with couscous. I don't think I knew what it was, but I knew I liked it the first time I tried it, in a cinderblock student dining hall at the *Université* in Aix-en-Provence. As a student at an American campus there, I could eat at the French *Université*—a "privilege" I exercised only on Fridays for that mountainous couscous. I doubt it was any better than college food usually is, but it was the only couscous I knew and I adored it. I still do, and I suspect that that first favorable taste of a world beyond rice launched my ongoing passion for grains.

I know I learned to love polenta as a cook at Chez Panisse in Berkeley, California, where I made gallons of it at a time. It was always enormously popular, whether topped with Gorgonzola or with a winey mushroom sauce. Polenta was becoming chic, a favorite with diners who would never dream of ordering cornmeal mush.

My father-in-law sold me on millet, a grain he religiously eats for breakfast as others take vitamin or fiber tablets. The first time

I stayed in his Oregon home and came downstairs for breakfast, I found him hunched over a bowl of something I'd never seen before.

"Thanks, but no thanks," I said to his offer of toast and eggs. "I'll have what you're having."

Like others, he had come to millet for health but found that it truly tasted good, especially with a little puddle of butter and maple syrup. Before the day was over, we'd driven down to the country store to buy me a sack of millet and a jar of that maple syrup.

Other cooks and favorite books have led me to other grains, while some I've bought and tried out of curiosity. For my money there's no better breakfast than hominy grits, rice pudding or buttered couscous. I love winter soups thickened with barley; spring peas in risotto; summer salads of parsley, tomatoes and bulgur; autumn game with wild rice.

I confess to love grains for their flavor but can't deny that their low cost and nutrition are selling points, too. How fortunate I am to hunger for foods that are good for me! Those who dream of hot fudge sundaes and then regret it when they've indulged should sit up and listen: Grains are guilt-free. Cultivate a taste for grains and your meals will be good for your health, kind to your purse and delicious.

Eight Great Grains

The eight grains featured in the chapters that follow are particular favorites. And I think they're becoming others' favorites, too. I find more *risotti* and *polenta* on Italian menus now; perhaps more telling, I spot them in restaurants that aren't Italian! Chefs are learning that polenta is as good with grilled ribs as it is with pure Italian sausage-and-peppers.

Cracked wheat and couscous are entering our repertoire, too, as chefs look to other countries for inspiration. If couscous is so good with all those spicy Moroccan stews, wouldn't it flatter some cinnamon-scented Greek lamb shanks? Iranians and Turks serve cracked wheat with skewered and spiced grilled lamb; why not serve it with herbed and grilled California lamb chops?

We're sure to be seeing more of hominy, barley and wild rice, too, as American chefs explore our own culinary past. What's more American than hominy grits or bacon-wrapped quail on wild rice?

SUBSTITUTIONS AND ADJUSTMENTS

Because many grains have similar texture and comparable flavor, they can readily replace each other in recipes. Cooking times and liquid additions may have to be adjusted, but many of the dishes in this book could be successfully made with a grain other than the one called for. Where appropriate, I've made recommendations for substitutions in some of the recipes.

f California plantings continue to grow, this luxury grain should become more affordable and better known.

Millet has an image problem, but perhaps it will benefit from Americans' increased interest in fiber. When properly cooked and seasoned, it is one of the tastiest grains on the shelf. Try it toasted in butter with scallions, like fried rice.

These eight grains and over 65 recipes are just a window on a much larger world. I hope you'll try these grains in dozens of other ways. I hope you're tempted to improvise and invent on your own. And I hope this little book piques your interest in the rest of the realm of grains.

'Tell Me What You Eat... "

Brillat-Savarin, the French philosopher/gastronome, professed to be able to read a man's character in his diet. "Tell me what you eat, and I will tell you what you are," he claimed.

Anyone who studies the world's cuisines can make a similar assertion: Tell me the grains you eat, and I will tell you who you are. For it's the Cantonese rice bowl, the Mexican tortilla and the loaf of French wheat bread that vividly symbolize the major distinction between these cuisines.

It is easy to see why grains became the foundation for most cuisines. As a protein source that is easily grown and stored, grains were immensely important to societies that couldn't count on a steady supply of meat or fish. Grains gave man the ability to sustain himself year-round. Once he learned to propagate them, however, he necessarily became tied to the land. He settled with others in stable communities and changed from a nomadic hunter/gatherer to an agrarian. Meats, fish and produce supplemented the diet when available, but the foundation of most ancient cooking was certainly grain.

In many parts of the world, it still is. Grains provide 80% of the calories consumed by man even today and take up half the arable land. They are made into flour, which is used for thickening, for breads and breadstuffs and for noodles. Grains are malted and made into grain alcohol the world over. Wherever meat and vegetables are scarce, grains provide nutritious means for stretching them. Even if there were the proverbial "chicken in every pot," the Mexican would shred his chicken and wrap it up in a tortilla, the Venetian would serve his with polenta, and the Japanese might stir his into a bowl of buckwheat noodles. From the Ethiopian *injera* (a fermented millet-flour pancake) to the bowl of southern cornmeal mush, grains are truly the "staff of life" all over the world.

Grain Anatomy

Botanically, grain kernels are seed-bearing fruits, containing all the genetic information for reproduction. Of the entire plant—be it wheat, corn or rice—we eat only this fruit or kernel. The kernels are made up of three main parts: the outer coat or "bran," which is high in fiber; the oil-rich seed or "germ"; and the starch- and protein-rich endosperm, often the only part of the grain we eat.

What happens to the grain between harvest and market—how and how much it is processed—affects flavor, nutrition and cooking qualities.

Processing Grains: How Groats Become Oats

Most grains require some degree of processing before they can be cooked. Rice and wild rice, barley and oats have a tough protective husk that must be removed. Wheat, corn and rye do not have a husk but are usually processed to make cooking quicker and chewing easier.

Grains that are merely husked (if a husk is present) but are processed no further are known as groats, whole grains or whole berries. Most natural-food stores carry a variety of these whole grains in bulk.

Although superior nutritionally, whole grains do have some drawbacks:

(1) They take longer to cook than processed grains. Brown rice, for example, takes about 40 minutes; white rice, about 20 minutes.

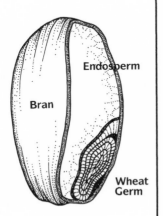

Endosperm

Bran

Wheat Germ

(2) They go rancid more quickly because they contain the oily germ. The deterioration is accelerated when the grain is ground into flour. (See Storing Grains, page 13.)

(3) Because the germ and bran get in the way of gluten production, whole-grain flour is harder to make into bread. Compare the difficulty of kneading a 100% whole wheat bread dough to the ease of kneading a 100% white flour dough.

(4) Whole grains have a full flavor that is inappropriate in some delicate dishes.

For these reasons and others, many grains are processed further by the following techniques:

Polishing or "pearling" with grooved rollers or carborundum stones is a way of scraping the grain enough to separate bran and germ from endosperm. Polished white rice and pearl barley are examples of grains that have undergone this treatment.

Cracking or coarse grinding the grain with steel blades or millstones makes it cook more quickly. In some cases, the whole grain (with bran and germ intact) is cracked; cracked rye and cracked wheat are made from whole grains. Other grains are polished first, then cracked; barley grits and hominy grits, for example, have been polished first.

Grinding reduces a grain to flour. Today most commercial grinding is done between steel rollers which generate heat in the process. To make whole wheat flour, bran and germ are removed, the endosperm is ground, then bran and germ are added back. Without this precaution, heat from the rollers would accelerate rancidity of the oil in the bran and germ. Stone-ground flours are usually ground between water-powered stones; many believe that this process is not as nutritionally damaging to the grain.

The grains included in this book have been processed to varying degrees:

Millet is a whole unpolished kernel.

Barley has been repeatedly "pearled" with abrasive carborundum wheels to remove its tough husk, bran and germ. After four to six pearlings, it is known as "pearl barley." "Pot barley" is available in some natural-food stores; it is more nutritious because it has had only a thin outer layer removed, but it must be soaked overnight and cooked longer. The recipes in this book were tested with pearl barley.

Arborio rice has been husked and polished.

Wild rice is a whole unpolished kernel.

Couscous is made from polished and ground wheat kernels.

Polenta is made from polished and ground dried corn.

Hominy and hominy grits are made from dried corn that has been hulled and degermed.

Cracked wheat is made from whole unpolished kernels.

Grains for the Health of It

The germ and bran together account for most of the fiber, oil and B vitamins, and about 25% of the protein, in grains. Whole grains are also a good source of such important trace minerals as chromium, manganese, copper, zinc, silenium and magnesium.

For most polished white rice, the vitamins lost during processing are added back. The rice is sprayed externally with a vitamin-enriched solution, then coated with protein powder and dried. That's why it's not a good idea (nutritionally) to wash polished rice—you wash away some of the vitamins and protein. However, some cooks prefer to sacrifice vitamins for texture; they claim that starchy residue on the rice will make the grains sticky if not rinsed off. Japanese rice is often coated with cornstarch and will be sticky if not rinsed before cooking. However, when making risotto, you definitely don't want to wash the grains because the surface starch will help make the dish creamy.

Grains are not a major protein source for meat-eating Westerners but they certainly are for other vegetable-eating peoples. Even today, grains and legumes together supply more than two-thirds of the world's dietary protein. In countries like India and China, grains are 70-80% of the caloric intake (about three times what they are in the West).

In the Western world, grain is especially valuable for its fiber content. Because we lack the enzyme to digest it, fiber is not available to us as an energy source as other complex carbohydrates are. Instead, it passes through the body, speeding up and easing digestion; it may also speed the elimination of carcinogens, thereby reducing the risk of colon or intestinal cancer. Although no direct causal relationship has been documented, scientists suspect a high-fiber diet can reduce the risk of several digestive-tract diseases. These benefits apply only to whole grains, with bran intact.

Storing Grains

All grains should be stored in tightly covered containers in a cool, dark, dry place. Heat, air and light accelerate rancidity. Whole grains, because they contain the oil-rich germ and bran (which go rancid first), have a shorter shelf life than degermed grains. Whole unpolished grains that have been cracked or ground, thereby exposing the germ, have an even shorter shelf life. Buy whole grains and processed whole grains (like cracked wheat) in small quantities; keep in a cool place or refrigerate. They have a shelf life of about four or five months. Polished grains (like Arborio rice and barley) should be kept cool and used within a year.

Grain Cookery Tips

Faced with an unfamiliar grain, most cooks have two main questions: How much liquid do I use and how long do I cook it? The following chart is a guide that can be adjusted to individual taste and intended use. To make a rice porridge, for example, you would cook the grain longer and with more liquid than the chart indicates. If you prefer a softer, less crunchy texture to millet, add more water and cook longer. Also, older grains are drier and may take longer to cook than young grains.

CHOOSE THE RIGHT POT

Remember that grains expand two to four times during cooking so choose a pot accordingly. For recipes that call for steaming the grain in a covered pot, make sure the pot has a tight-fitting lid. Heavy-bottomed pots are best for slow-cooked dishes like risotto and polenta because the food won't scorch as easily

1 CUP GRAIN	AMOUNT OF LIQUID	COOKING TIME	SPECIAL INSTRUCTIONS	COOKED YIELD
MILLET	1½ cups	15 minutes	Set aside, covered, for 10 minutes	4 cups
BARLEY	2½ cups	35 minutes		3½ cups
ARBORIO RICE (Risotto)	3 cups or more	20-25 minutes		2¾ cups
WILD RICE	6 cups	30 minutes	Drain and steam over liquid 15 for minutes	3 cups
COUSCOUS	1 cup	5 minutes		2 cups
POLENTA	4 cups	20-25 minutes		4 cups
HOMINY	See Basic Hominy (page 68)			
HOMINY GRITS (Regular)	4 cups	20 minutes		4 cups
HOMINY GRITS (Quick Cooking)	4 cups	6–7 minutes		4 cups
CRACKED WHEAT (Pilaf)	2 cups	15–20 minutes		2¾ cups
CRACKED WHEAT (Porridge)	4 cups	20 minutes		3 cups

Vary Liquids for Flavor

The more flavorful the liquid you use in grain cookery, the more flavorful the finished dish. All grains may be cooked in water, but most savory grain dishes are improved with the use of stock. Porridge-type grain dishes are occasionally cooked in milk or a water/milk mixture for added richness.

COOK'S NOTE

Several of the recipes in this book call for chicken stock. A medium-strength homemade chicken stock is preferred, but canned chicken stock is fine if watered down to an acceptable strength and salt level.

About Sprouts

Because grains incorporate seeds with all the equipment for reproduction, they are easy to germinate. When kept in a warm, dark, wet environment, the embryo (germ) begins converting the grain's starch into energy for growth. It "sprouts" and puts forth a root.

Many people enjoy sprouts' nutty, sweet flavor and use them to add crunch to salads and breads. Others buy sprouts for their perceived nutritional benefits. Scientists are still not sure exactly how sprouting alters the nutritional makeup of a grain. They do know that sprouts have considerably more Vitamin C than the unsprouted seed—but that's still not very much. They also have fewer calories because they burn up carbohydrates in the process of sprouting.

To Sprout Whole Grains, first wash the grains well, then put them in a bowl with 4 parts warm (70° to 80°F.) water to 1 part grains. Cover bowl with plastic wrap and let stand overnight. Drain sprouts well and divide among clean quart jars, putting about ¼ cup soaked grains in each jar. Cover jars with a double thickness of damp cheesecloth and fix it to the rim with a rubber band. Set jars in a warm dark place. Twice a day, fill jar with tepid water, swish to coat all the grains, then let water drain off through the cheesecloth and return jar to resting place. Continue until beans produce sprouts of desired length, usually about 3 to 5 days.

Arborio Rice

Arborio Rice

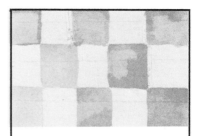

Northern Italy's rice growers produce several varieties of short-grain rice, but the one most exported is Arborio. Arborio rice is at and stubby, with a white spot on the kernel. Its distinguishing feature is its high content of amylopectin, a component of starch that gelatinizes readily.

Consequently, Arborio rice makes lovely puddings and is a necessity for the creamy rice dishes of Northern Italy known as *risotti*. When cooked slowly in a little liquid, it doesn't split open like a long-grain rice; instead, it swells gently and its surface starch forms a creamy sauce.

Like pasta preparations, Italian *risotti* reflect the seasons. In the late spring, the first peas might prompt Risotto with Peas and Pancetta (page 23). In autumn weather, Duck Risotto (page 26) or a Risotto with Meat Broth and Marrow (page 24) would be more appealing.

Arborio rice is delicious in soups because of the creamy way it swells as it cooks. Add it to vegetable-filled Minestrone Verde (page 5) or to a winter cabbage soup. In rice puddings, Arborio gives a wonderful clinging texture. Flavor the pudding in the Indian style with rosewater and pistachios (page 29), or make it with vanilla and a crackling burnt sugar crust (page 30).

A JUNE DINNER PARTY

Here's a dinner-party menu for late spring to early summer, when both peas and strawberries are at their peak. If you're serving two wines, consider a rich Chardonnay with the risotto and a light Pinot Noir or Chianti with the veal; otherwise, pour the red wine throughout.

Risotto with Meat Broth and Marrow (page 24)

Broiled Veal Chops with Rosemary

Buttered Spring Peas

Strawberries with Sugar and Balsamic Vinegar

Basic Risotto

A true Italian risotto requires Arborio rice and patience. Due to its amylopectin content (see page 19), Arborio swells and sticks together as it cooks. For those of us brought up in the "separate grain" school of rice cookery, the idea seems heretical. But one taste of a creamy risotto confirms that the dish can be properly made with nothing else.

It takes patience to stir the risotto throughout the 25-minute cooking process, but stirring keeps it from burning or sticking to the bottom of the pot. And it takes practice to master the timing so that the rice is tender and creamy when all the liquid is used up. Each batch of rice can take a little more or a little less liquid, depending on its processing and its age. The important point is to add the liquid a little at a time, adding more only when the previous addition has been absorbed. The result should be very creamy, a bit thicker than a soup, but not by much.

Risotto is a first course in Italy and is garnished with whatever strikes the cook's fancy. You can almost follow the seasons by following the risotti on restaurant menus. In spring it's offered with asparagus tips or artichoke hearts; in summer with peas, zucchini, zucchini flowers or basil; in autumn with autumn mushrooms or truffles; and in winter with shellfish.

As much as I love risotto, I have a hard time working it into dinner party menus given the tight configuration of my home. If I plan it as a first course, either I spend 25 minutes alone in the kitchen while my guests have aperitifs in the living room, or I ask them to keep me company while I stand and stir. The latter solution only works when we're entertaining one other couple; beyond that, it gets too crowded in the kitchen. Sometimes it works out better to have risotto as a second or main course. Since the dining table is in the kitchen, I can cook and still be part of the conversation. You'll have to work out a solution that fits your situation. Just remember that risotto must be stirred constantly and served when it's done. It cannot be successfully held.

BUYER'S NOTE

Arborio rice is widely available in Italian markets, specialty stores and some well-stocked supermarkets. Other short-grain rice varieties will work in the following recipes, but Arborio will give the most authentic *risotti* and the most pleasing texture. Other short-grain Italian rice varieties that are occasionally available include Vialone Nano, a grain smaller than Arborio and considered slightly inferior; and Carnaroli, a superior and more expensive grain in short supply.

Melt butter in a heavy-bottomed 4-quart saucepan. Add onions and sauté over moderate heat until softened, about 5 minutes. Add rice and stir to coat well. Sauté, stirring constantly, for 2 minutes.

Bring stock to a simmer in a separate saucepan. Add hot stock to rice ½ cup at a time, stirring constantly with a wooden spoon and waiting until each ½ cup of stock is almost fully absorbed before adding another. It should take about 25 minutes for rice to absorb stock and become tender. At that point, *risotto* should be creamy, not soupy or gummy. Season with salt and pepper and stir in the Parmesan.

Divide *risotto* among warm bowls and dust each serving with minced parsley. Serve with additional Parmesan on the side.

Makes 4 servings.

3 Tb. unsalted butter

1 cup chopped onions

1½ cups Arborio rice

About 5 cups chicken or veal stock (see COOK'S NOTE, page 14)

Salt and freshly ground black pepper

¼ cup freshly grated Parmesan cheese, plus additional for serving

2 Tb. minced parsley

Risotto Verde
Green Risotto

To make an easy variation on a basic risotto, try adding a paste of garlic, basil, spinach and parsley. The result is highly aromatic and makes a delicious summer first course before a grilled swordfish or salmon.

4 Tb. unsalted butter

2 large cloves garlic

½ cup loosely packed fresh basil leaves

1½ cups loosely packed fresh spinach, stems removed

½ cup loosely packed parsley, stems removed

1 small onion, chopped

1½ cups Arborio rice

About 5 cups chicken stock (see COOK'S NOTE, page 14)

¼ cup freshly grated Parmesan cheese, plus additional for serving

Salt and freshly ground black pepper

Bring 2 tablespoons butter to room temperature. Combine garlic, basil, spinach and parsley in a food processor or blender and blend to a near-paste. Add softened butter, blend well and set aside.

Melt remaining 2 tablespoons butter in a heavy-bottomed 4-quart saucepan over moderate heat. Add onion and sauté until softened, about 5 minutes. Add rice and stir to coat well. Sauté, stirring constantly, for 2 minutes. Bring chicken stock to a simmer in a separate saucepan. Add hot stock to rice ½ cup at a time, stirring constantly with a wooden spoon and waiting until each ½ cup of stock is almost fully absorbed before adding another. It should take about 25 minutes for rice to absorb stock and become tender. At this point, the risotto should be creamy, not soupy or gummy.

Stir in herb paste and the Parmesan. Season to taste with salt and pepper. Serve immediately in warm bowls. Pass extra Parmesan.

Makes 4 servings.

Risotto with Peas and Pancetta

Wherever hogs are raised, there are frugal cooks who know how to use every last part. The same belly section that Americans smoke for bacon is made into pancetta in Italy: It's salt-cured—not smoked—seasoned with pepper and rolled like a jelly roll.

Sliced, diced and rendered to crispness, it's a delicious last-minute addition to a creamy risotto with spring peas.

Render pancetta slowly in a large skillet until crisp; transfer with a slotted spoon to paper towels to drain.

If using fresh peas, steam them in a little boiling water until just tender, 5 to 10 minutes. Drain well and set aside. If using frozen peas, simply defrost.

Melt 3 tablespoons butter in a heavy-bottomed 4-quart saucepan. Add scallions and sauté over moderate heat until slightly softened, about 3 minutes. Add rice and stir to coat well. Sauté, stirring constantly, for 2 minutes.

Bring stock to a simmer in a separate saucepan. Add hot stock to rice ½ cup at a time, stirring constantly with a wooden spoon and waiting until each ½ cup of stock is almost fully absorbed before adding another. It should take about 25 minutes for the rice to absorb all the stock and become tender. At that point, the *risotto* should be creamy, not soupy or gummy.

Stir in peas, pancetta and remaining tablespoon butter. Season with salt and pepper. Divide *risotto* among four warm bowls. Serve Parmesan on the side.

Makes 4 servings.

½ pound pancetta, diced
¾ cup shelled peas, fresh or frozen
4 Tb. unsalted butter
¾ cup sliced scallions
1½ cups Arborio rice
5 cups chicken stock (see COOK'S NOTE, page 14)
Salt and freshly ground black pepper
Freshly grated Parmesan cheese, for serving

Risotto with Meat Broth and Marrow

Inside every beef shank bone, and running the length of the bone, is a narrow strip of firm white marrow. If you roast the bones briefly, the marrow turns soft and creamy. It can then be lifted out easily and added to risotto for extra richness. Marrow melts almost as easily as butter, so stir it in at the last minute to retain its smooth texture. Any butcher should be willing to saw shank bones in half for you.

2 marrow (beef shank) bones, 6 to 8 inches long, split in half lengthwise
3 Tb. unsalted butter
2 cups thinly sliced leeks
1½ cups Arborio rice
5 cups homemade veal stock
Salt and freshly ground black pepper
2 Tb. minced parsley
¼ cup freshly grated Parmesan cheese, plus additional for serving

Preheat oven to 300°F.

Put the marrow bones, split side up, in a shallow roasting pan and roast 10 minutes. Set aside until cool enough to handle. Use a narrow spoon or a table knife to slip the marrow out of its cavity, in one piece if possible. Reserve.

Melt butter in a heavy-bottomed 4-quart saucepan. Add leeks and sauté over moderate heat until slightly softened, about 4 minutes. Add rice and stir to coat well with butter. Sauté, stirring constantly, for 2 minutes.

Bring stock to a simmer in a separate saucepan. Add the hot stock to the rice ½ cup at a time, stirring constantly with a wooden spoon and waiting until each ½ cup of stock is almost fully absorbed before adding another. It should take about 25 minutes for the rice to absorb all the stock and become tender. At that point, the *risotto* should be creamy, not soupy or gummy. Season with salt and pepper and stir in parsley.

Slice the marrow ¼-inch thick and carefully stir it into the risotto. Divide *risotto* among four warm bowls and grate Parmesan over each serving.

Makes 4 servings.

Minestrone Verde
Minestrone with Green Vegetables

his light spring minestrone can be made in half an hour and can be endlessly varied to suit what you find in the market. Replace the zucchini with tender string beans, replace the fava beans with peas, replace cabbage with escarole or chard—it doesn't matter. Just be sure that all the vegetables are cut such that they'll cook in about the same time. The soup is meant to be thick with rice.

Heat oil in a 4-quart pot over moderate heat. Add garlic and red pepper flakes and sauté until fragrant, about 1 minute.

Add zucchini, celery, leeks, cabbage, fennel, fava beans and rice and stir to coat with oil. Add ham and broth and bring to a boil. Cover, reduce heat and simmer until rice is just tender, about 12 minutes.

Remove ham hock, chop meat coarsely and return meat to soup. Remove soup from heat, stir in mint and season to taste with salt and pepper. Cover and let stand 5 minutes. Serve with plenty of Parmesan.

Makes 6 servings.

2 Tb. vegetable oil
3 cloves garlic, minced
Pinch hot red pepper flakes
2 small zucchini, diced
1 cup diced celery
¾ cup sliced leeks
¼ head medium cabbage, coarsely shredded
1 medium bulb fennel, cored and sliced thin
8 ounces fresh shelled fava beans
1½ cups Arborio rice
6 ounces smoked ham hock, in one piece
8 cups chicken stock (see COOK'S NOTE, page 14)
2 Tb. minced fresh mint
Salt and freshly ground black pepper
Freshly grated Parmesan cheese

Duck Risotto

When I stopped cooking at Chez Panisse, I started writing about food. For one of my first articles, I took a basket of groceries to three local chefs and asked them to make a meal using only what they'd been given.

Alice Waters of Chez Panisse made a wonderful duck risotto, using every inch of the bird: the wings, legs, neck and carcass were made into stock; the breasts, liver and gizzard were browned and stirred into the rice; and the duck skin was rendered for a crisp garnish. What follows is my recollection of her method.

This is a main course risotto, to serve with a red Burgundy or a Pinot Noir.

One 5-pound fresh
duck, with feet and
neck attached
4 slices thick-cut bacon
1 large onion, coarsely
chopped
2 bay leaves
12 black peppercorns
4 Tb. unsalted butter
2 cups thinly sliced leeks
1½ cups Arborio rice
Salt and freshly ground
black pepper
2 Tb. minced parsley

Clean duck inside and out, removing any visible fat deposits. Reserve liver and gizzard. Cut off and reserve wings, legs, feet and neck (fig. 1), then carefully remove breasts from carcass (fig. 2). Chop carcass into four pieces (fig. 3).

Cut bacon slices into ½-inch widths. Render bacon in a large stockpot until almost crisp. Pour off accumulated fat, saving it for another use. Add onion and duck wings, legs, feet, neck and carcass to stockpot. Brown over moderately high heat, about 15 minutes. Add bay leaves, peppercorns and 3 quarts water. Bring to a boil slowly, skimming carefully, then reduce heat and simmer for 3 hours.

Strain stock into a clean bowl and discard solids. Refrigerate stock overnight, if possible, to allow fat to rise to the top. If you are not making the stock ahead, let it rest at least 30 minutes and spoon off as much surface fat as possible.

Heat a skillet until medium hot. Salt and pepper duck breasts well, and put them skin side down in the skillet (no additional fat is necessary). Brown about 4 minutes, then turn and cook an additional 2 to 3 minutes. Transfer breasts to a plate; when cool enough to handle, carefully peel away skin.

Cut skin into ½-inch squares and add to skillet over low heat. Render skin slowly, pouring off fat as it accumulates. When pieces are reduced to small, brown, crisp "cracklings", remove them with a slotted spoon to paper towels. When they are completely cool, chop them coarsely and set aside.

Melt 1 tablespoon butter in a small skillet over moderate

heat and sauté duck liver and gizzard until they are pink throughout. Season with salt and pepper and set aside.

Melt 3 tablespoons butter in a heavy-bottomed 2-quart pot. Add leeks and sauté over moderate heat until softened, about 5 minutes. Add rice and stir to coat well. Cook, stirring constantly, for 2 minutes. Bring 5 cups duck stock to a simmer in a separate saucepan. Add hot stock to rice ½ cup at a time, stirring constantly with a wooden spoon and waiting until each ½ cup of stock is almost fully absorbed before adding another. It should take about 25 minutes for rice to absorb all the stock and become tender. At that point, the *risotto* should be creamy, not soupy or gummy.

Slice duck breast against the grain into neat strips; slice livers and gizzard into small pieces. Season *risotto* with salt and pepper; stir in parsley, then stir in duck breast, livers and gizzard at the last minute. Divide *risotto* among four warm bowls and top each portion with rendered duck skin.

Makes 4 servings.

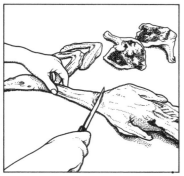

fig. 1

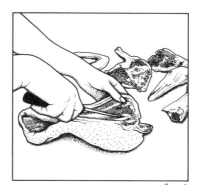

fig. 2

1. Cut off wings, legs, feet and neck.

2. Remove breast from carcass.

fig. 3

fig. 4

3. Chop carcass into four pieces.

4. The duck parts.

Insalata di Riso
Italian Rice Salad

The Italians serve rice salad as part of a summer antipasto or as the main course of a dog-day lunch. Surround it with wedges of tomato and hard-cooked egg to make a handsome platter, and follow it with sliced sugared peaches in white wine.

4 cups water
Pinch salt
1 cup Arborio rice
1 Tb. olive oil
⅓ cup homemade
   mayonnaise
3 anchovy fillets,
   minced
2 Tb. minced parsley
3 Tb. minced red
   pepper, roasted and
   peeled
1½ Tb. capers
1 to 2 Tb. tarragon
   vinegar
⅓ to ½ pound cooked
   shrimp, coarsely
   chopped
Salt and freshly ground
   black pepper

Bring water and salt to a boil in a large saucepan. Add rice, stir with a fork and reduce heat to maintain a simmer. Simmer, uncovered, 15 minutes, stirring occasionally at first to keep rice from sticking to the bottom of the pan. When rice is just tender to the bite, drain well in a sieve or colander and stir in olive oil. Set aside to cool.

In a large bowl, combine mayonnaise, anchovies, parsley, red pepper, capers and 1 tablespoon tarragon vinegar. Stir to blend. Add cooled rice and stir with a fork until well blended. Stir in shrimp. Season to taste with salt and pepper and add more vinegar if desired.

Makes 6 servings as part of an antipasto platter.

Rice Pudding with Rosewater and Pistachios

For centuries Middle Eastern cooks have used the essence of flowers to flavor their dishes. Rosewater, in particular, has an unforgettable perfume that makes something exotic out of something as prosaic as rice pudding. Serve this pudding after a meal with a Middle Eastern or Indian flavor—say, a butterflied grilled leg of lamb served with mint relish, or a roast chicken basted with butter and saffron.

Combine milk, sugar, salt and rice in top of a large double boiler. Place over barely simmering water and cook, uncovered, for about 2 hours, stirring occasionally and scraping down sides of pan with a spatula. After about 1½ hours, pudding will begin to thicken noticeably; stir often during the last 30 minutes. When pudding is thick and creamy and rice is tender, remove pan from heat. Let cool 5 minutes, then stir in rosewater to taste.

Pour rice pudding into a serving dish or divide it among four individual dishes. Serve hot, or refrigerate and serve chilled. Just before serving, top pudding with pistachios.

Makes 4 servings.

4 cups milk
⅓ cup sugar
Scant ½ tsp. salt
½ cup Arborio rice
1 to 1½ tsp. rosewater
¼ cup shelled unsalted pistachios, lightly toasted and minced

Vanilla Rice Pudding with Burnt Sugar Crust

*W*hoever originated Burnt Cream was surely divinely inspired. Putting a crackling sheet of caramel atop a cold, creamy custard was an idea that ranks right up there with Eskimo Pies. The same idea works well with a creamy rice pudding, too, and is a clever way to dress up a homespun dessert.

4 cups milk
⅓ cup sugar
½ cup Arborio rice
Scant ½ tsp. salt
2 egg yolks
½ tsp. pure vanilla
  extract
Granulated sugar

Combine milk, sugar, rice and salt in top of a large double boiler. Place over barely simmering water and cook, uncovered, for about 2 hours, stirring occasionally and scraping down sides of pan with a spatula. After about 1½ hours, pudding will begin to thicken noticeably; stir often during the last 30 minutes.

Five minutes before rice is done, beat egg yolks slightly in a bowl. Stir in a little hot rice to warm the eggs, then add eggs to pudding mixture. Stir well and cook, stirring constantly, until pudding thickens, about 5 more minutes. Remove from heat; let cool slightly, then stir in vanilla. Divide mixture among six ovenproof custard cups or ramekins. Chill thoroughly.

At least two hours before serving, preheat broiler and place oven rack in uppermost position. Arrange custard cups on a tray. Top each with a ⅛-inch-thick layer of sugar, patting the sugar into a perfectly even layer. If the layer is not even, the sugar will burn in some places before it caramelizes in others. Place tray under broiler and watch constantly. Sugar will quickly bubble, melt and caramelize. When sugar is a deep caramel color all over, remove tray and refrigerate pudding. Serve pudding well chilled.

Makes 6 servings.

Barley

Barley

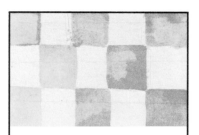

Most of America's barley goes to cows, pigs and breweries, with only 20 percent of the crop left for soups and stews. The rest of the world knows better: Foreign cooks use barley in everything from the soup course to dessert.

The Chinese use barley and lotus seeds as a stuffing for duck. The Japanese make a cold "tea" from roasted barley. Scandinavian cooks make barley into breakfast porridges and dessert puddings. Indian cooks add barley flour to breads. English nannies feed barley water to their wards for their constitution; English ladies drink it for their complexion. But the Scots are probably the world's greatest appreciators of the grain, for it's the foundation of their world-famous whiskey.

Most of the barley available in our markets has been "pearled" to remove the tough hull. Pearling involves a series of trips through revolving abrasive disks. Three pearlings are sufficient to remove the hull and some of the bran, producing what is known as "pot barley." But most of the barley in our markets has had five or six pearlings, removing hull, bran and even some of the germ. It is usually labeled "pearl barley."

Obviously, pearling removes vitamins and minerals, but if you cooked unpearled barley long enough to soften its chewy hull, you wouldn't have many nutrients left either. Even pot barley must be soaked overnight to soften it before cooking. The recipes in this chapter were tested with pearl barley.

The first-time barley cook is always amazed at how much it expands. Put a cup in two quarts of broth and watch it grow. The grain almost quadruples. Think before you add, or you'll end up with a little soup in your barley instead of a little barley in your soup.

A DUCK DINNER

A crisp-skinned duck simply seasoned with salt and pepper is a good match for oven-baked barley. For a spring dinner, precede it with asparagus and follow with rhubarb. In the fall, you might start with a chicory salad and end with an an apple or pear dessert.

Chilled Asparagus with Tarragon Mayonnaise

Roast Duck

*Barley, Bacon and Peppers
(page 39)*

Rhubarb Crisp

Basic Barley

I like plain steamed barley for breakfast with a little butter, brown sugar and cream. (See Breakfast Barley, page 35, for a creamy version.) For dinner, you could top it with lamb stew or creamed mushrooms; or you could toss the cooked grains with buttered peas and dill and serve it with broiled lamb chops. Basic steamed barley can be stirred into soups for added body and texture. For a more flavorful dish, substitute chicken or veal stock for all or part of the water.

2½ cups water
1 cup pearl barley
Salt and freshly ground
   black pepper
Butter, optional

Bring lightly salted water to a boil in a saucepan. Add barley, stir once and cover. Reduce heat to low and cook until water is absorbed and grain is tender, about 35 minutes. Season to taste with salt and pepper. Add butter if desired.

Makes about 3½ cups.

BUYER'S NOTE

Most supermarkets carry pearl barley, sometimes called soup barley, in plastic bags. Natural-food stores are a good source for pearl and pot barley in bulk. Some natural-food stores also carry barley grits (ground pearl barley) in coarse, medium or fine sizes. Barley grits can be simmered to make a breakfast porridge or steamed to make a savory side dish.

Breakfast Barley

I do love hot cereal on cold winter mornings, but I don't want to wait an hour for it. With grains like barley that take a long time to cook, I'll often make a large pot one evening, then re-heat it all week with a little milk.

Bring water, sugar and salt to a boil in a 1½-quart saucepan over high heat. Add barley, cover and reduce heat to low. Cook until barley is tender and liquid is absorbed, about 1 hour. Five min-utes before barley is done, stir in currants or raisins.

Divide cereal between two warm bowls. Put a teaspoon of butter in the center of each portion. Sprinkle with Cinnamon Sugar and serve with a pitcher of cream, half-and-half or milk.

Makes 2 servings.

2 cups water
1 Tb. sugar
¼ tsp. salt
½ cup pearl barley
¼ cup currants or
    raisins
2 tsp. unsalted butter
Cinnamon Sugar: 2
    tablespoons sugar and
    ½ teaspoon cinnamon
Cream or milk

Leek and Barley Soup

Barley is popular in Scandinavia because it matures in the rel-atively short growing season. Danes enjoy it in soups and porridge. Often they cook it with buttermilk and crown it with cool summer berries.

Fresh dill and sour cream give this soup its Scandinavian flavor. Serve it as a Sunday supper with black bread and soft cheese.

Melt butter in a large saucepan. Add leeks and sauté, stirring often, until softened, about 15 minutes. Add chicken stock and bring to a simmer. Add barley and cook, uncovered, until barley is tender, about 45 minutes. Add salt and pepper to taste. Stir in fresh dill. Serve hot, garnished with a dollop of sour cream.

Makes 6 servings.

3 Tb. unsalted butter
6 cups thinly sliced leeks
8 cups chicken stock
    (see COOK'S NOTE,
    page 14)
⅔ cup pearl barley
Salt and freshly ground
    black pepper
2 Tb. minced fresh dill
Sour cream, whisked
    until smooth

Scotch Broth

I t's a meal-in-a-bowl, devised for mean Scottish winters but tasty whenever and wherever the weather turns foul. The Scots may make it with mutton, but the American taste is for younger lamb. Just be sure to use cuts—like neck and shoulder—that have plenty of fat and flavor. The vegetables listed are merely suggestions: split peas or fresh peas, rutabagas or parsnips can be added or substituted. The soup is best started a day ahead so you can chill the broth and easily lift off the congealed fat.

4 pounds lamb neck and shoulder

¾ cup pearl barley

4 slices bacon, in ½-inch widths

2 small onions, coarsely chopped

3 small carrots, coarsely chopped

3 ribs celery, in ½-inch widths

2 medium turnips, peeled and cubed

½ head small cabbage, coarsely shredded

Salt and freshly ground black pepper

Put lamb in a large stockpot and add 4 quarts cold water. Bring slowly to a boil, skimming frequently, then reduce heat and simmer for 2½ hours, skimming as necessary. Strain stock into a clean container and refrigerate overnight.

When meat is cool enough to handle, remove and discard any bones and large pieces of fat. You should have about 3 cups coarsely shredded meat. Put it into a plastic container, spoon a little stock over it and refrigerate overnight.

The next day, lift off and discard the congealed fat from the surface of the stock. Bring stock to a simmer, add barley and cook 20 minutes. In a separate stockpot, render bacon until almost crisp. Add onions, carrots, celery and turnips and cook over moderately high heat, stirring often, until vegetables begin to brown. Add barley and stock and continue simmering until vegetables and barley are tender. Five minutes before they are done, stir in cabbage and reserved meat. Season to taste with salt and pepper.

Makes 8 servings.

Lima Bean and Barley Soup

Beef, *beans and barley are a common threesome in Slavic soups, with the amount of beef reflecting the state of the budget. Use a fatty cut—short ribs or flank—for maximum flavor and body and make sure your paprika is fresh and lively. This humble soup is a winter dinner to have with a full-bodied beer.*

Bring lima beans and water to a boil in a saucepan. Boil one minute, then cover and remove from heat. Let stand one hour. Or soak lima beans in water overnight.

Heat oil in a large heavy-bottomed stockpot over medium-high heat. Add short ribs and brown well on all sides. Pour off all fat and return pot to low heat. Add butter and onion and sauté until softened, about 10 minutes. Add lima beans and their water to the pot. Bring to a boil, cover and reduce heat to maintain a simmer. Simmer slowly one hour. Add barley, cover and cook 45 minutes more.

Remove meat from stockpot. When cool enough to handle, remove and discard any fat or gristle and chop the meat coarsely. Return it to the pot along with paprika and salt and pepper to taste. Stir in chopped chives just before serving. Offer sour cream, if desired.

Makes 8 cups, about 6 servings.

1 cup dried lima beans
7 cups water
2 Tb. olive oil
1 pound beef short ribs, in three pieces
1 Tb. unsalted butter
1 large onion, coarsely chopped
¾ cup pearl barley
½ tsp. Hungarian paprika
Salt and freshly ground black pepper
2 Tb. chopped fresh chives
Sour cream, optional

Barley and Bow Ties

Kasha varnishkes—*buckwheat groats and broad noodles—is a fixture on Jewish Sabbath tables, usually served with a juicy brisket or a plump roast chicken. The version below calls for barley and the fat, frilly "bowtie" noodles that Italians call farfalle ("butterflies"). Cracked wheat could be substituted for barley, although you'd have to shorten the cooking time and reduce the volume of cooking liquid (see chart, page 14).*

1 cup pearl barley
1 cup minced onion
½ pound mushrooms, sliced
1½ Tb. unsalted butter
Salt and freshly ground black pepper
¼ tsp. paprika
4 ounces dried pasta bowties or *farfalle*
Melted butter
Minced parsley, optional

Bring 2½ cups salted water to boil in a saucepan. Add barley, stir once and cover. Reduce heat to low and cook 35 minutes.

Meanwhile, sauté onion and mushrooms in butter over high heat, stirring often, until they soften, about 10 minutes. Season with salt, pepper and paprika.

Cook pasta according to package directions; drain well and toss with a little melted butter to keep bowties from sticking.

When barley is done, transfer to a warm serving bowl; add mushroom/onion mixure and bowties and toss lightly to blend. Taste and adjust seasoning. Garnish with parsley, if desired.

Makes 4 generous servings.

Barley, Bacon and Peppers

*S**weet peppers and barley go together like peaches and cream. Stuff peppers with barley. Stir-fry peppers and barley. Or make this pilaf with peppers, barley and smoky bacon. Serve the pilaf as a partner to roast duck or quail, to pork or veal chops or lamb brochettes.***

Preheat oven to 375°F.

Render bacon in an ovenproof 10-inch skillet over moderate heat until crisp. Transfer bacon with a slotted spoon to paper towels to drain. Pour off all but one tablespoon fat. Add red and green bell pepper and sauté over moderately high heat until slightly softened, about 5 minutes. Add barley and stir to coat well.

Bring chicken stock or water to a boil and add to skillet along with rendered bacon. Stir, cover and place skillet in oven. Cook until all liquid is absorbed and barley is tender, about 1 hour. Uncover and fluff with a fork. Add salt, if necessary, and season generously with black pepper.

Makes 4 to 6 servings.

3 slices bacon, cut crosswise into ¼-inch widths

¾ cup minced red bell pepper

¾ cup minced green bell pepper

1 cup pearl barley

3 cups chicken stock or water (see COOK'S NOTE, page 14)

Salt and freshly ground black pepper

Braised Oxtails and Barley

I f the best meat is next to the bone, as it's said, then oxtails ought to be one of the choicest cuts on the steer. Indeed they are! Braised slowly and for several hours, the meat turns succulent and tender, and the bones yield their gelatin to the sauce. In the dish below, barley is added halfway through to plump in the oxtail juices. A little star anise imparts a mysterious clovelike scent, with a shower of lemon rind, parsley and garlic to heighten the flavors. This is a splendid party dish—inexpensive, easy, and entirely do-able ahead. It looks delectable in its casserole and it makes the house smell great. Serve a Zinfandel or, better yet, a good ale.

3 pounds oxtails
Salt and freshly ground
    black pepper
2 Tb. vegetable oil
2 medium onions, sliced
1 tsp. Hungarian
    paprika
4 cups beef stock
7 points star anise
1 cup pearl barley
¼ cup minced parsley
1 tsp. grated lemon rind
1 clove garlic, minced

Have butcher saw oxtails into chunks about 1½ inches in diameter. Season with salt and pepper. Heat 1 tablespoon oil in a large, heavy skillet. Brown oxtails well, in batches if necessary, and transfer to a large ovenproof casserole.

Pour off and discard any fat remaining in skillet, then add remaining tablespoon oil. Add onions and paprika and sauté over moderately high heat until onions have softened slightly, about 5 minutes. Transfer onions to casserole.

Deglaze the skillet over high heat with 1 cup stock, scraping the bottom of the skillet with a wooden spoon to loosen any browned bits. Transfer liquid to casserole along with another 2 cups stock and star anise.

Preheat oven to 325°F.

Bring casserole to a simmer on top of the stove, then cover and bake in the preheated oven for 1½ hours. Remove casserole from oven and strain off any liquid into a large measuring cup or bowl. Remove and discard anise points from liquid and carefully spoon off the fat that rises to the surface of the cup. Return liquid to casserole and stir in barley and remaining cup of stock. Cover and cook until barley is tender, about 1½ hours more.

Combine parsley, lemon rind and garlic. Transfer braised oxtails and barley to a warm serving bowl (or serve from the casserole) and sprinkle with parsley mixture just before serving.

Makes 4 servings.

Couscous

Couscous

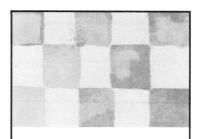

Remove the bran and germ from a kernel of hard durum wheat and you're left with the endosperm, a.k.a. semolina (see illustration, page 10). When ground, it yields high-protein, high-gluten semolina flour, the basis of Italy's dried pasta and the basis of couscous.

To make couscous, semolina flour is mixed with salted water, then tossed and rubbed into distinct tiny pellets. The pellets are then steamed twice over simmering water until they soften and swell; often, the second steaming takes place over a bubbling stew.

Couscous is fundamental to the diets of Moroccans, Algerians, Tunisians and Egyptians. In North Africa, the word "couscous" describes not only the steamed grain, but a whole category of dishes made of couscous, stewed meats and steamed vegetables. In southern France, home to many immigrant North Africans, couscous is a popular offering in the low-priced student restaurants. The dish has also made its way to Paris, where going out to a neighborhood restaurant for couscous is not uncommon.

Enjoy it as a breakfast cereal (see Couscous Cream of Wheat, page 46), as a side dish with grilled meats (see Couscous with Curry Butter, Pistachios and Currants, page 48), as the foundation for a stew (see Couscous with Greek-Style Lamb Shanks, page 52) or as an addition to soup (see Moroccan-Style Chicken Soup, page 47). Sprinkled with cinnamon-sugar and nuts, it's a delicious dessert.

AN AUTUMN DINNER

I think of a hearty, meaty stew as the centerpiece of an autumn menu, with a simple salad before and a fruit dessert after. Like most stews, the one below improves with reheating, which makes it a good choice for days when you've invited guests for dinner but know you won't have time to cook.

Spinach, Onion and Feta Salad

Couscous with Greek-style Lamb Shanks (page 52)

Sliced Oranges in Pomegranate Juice

Basic Couscous

*E*xpertly steamed couscous is light and fluffy, with each grain soft and separate. It's not hard to do, but it does take some time and it helps to have the right equipment. Although couscous can be steamed in a colander set over a pot of simmering water, a couscousière makes the job a lot easier.

The traditional couscousière looks something like a double boiler, but the bottom half is narrow and deep, and the top half pierced with tiny holes (fig. 1). Initially, water goes into the bottom half and couscous goes into the top; the contraption is placed over heat and the couscous swells, uncovered, in the rising steam. For the final (second) steaming, the water in the bottom of the pot is replaced by a bubbling stew, and the couscous cooks in the flavorful juices swirling up from underneath.

Because the two parts fit so neatly together, a couscousière makes the cooking easy. If you have to jerryrig a steamer with colander and kettle, you'll have to make sure the steam cannot escape out the sides, possibly by sealing the circumference with a wet dishtowel or length of cheesecloth (fig. 2). The full force of the steam is what makes the couscous grains swell as they should.

1. The couscousière.

2. Cheesecloth wrapped around the couscousière.

fig. 1

fig. 2

Put the couscous in a rimmed baking dish, approximately 13 by 9 inches. Cover with 4½ cups cold water. Swish the water through quickly, "raking" the grains with your fingers, then drain the couscous in a sieve.

Return grains to the baking dish and smooth them out with your fingers. Let stand 15 minutes. Break the grains up gently with your fingers, then rub them lightly between the palms of your hands to break up any lumps.

When all visible lumps have been broken up, put about 3 inches of water in the bottom half of the *couscousière* and cover with the top half. Cut a piece of cheesecloth a little longer than the circumference of the top of the bottom half; wet it and squeeze it dry, then dust it lightly with flour. Wrap it securely around the *couscousière* where the top and bottom halves join (fig. 2). You want to make sure the steam cannot escape except through the holes in the top half.

Set the pot over high heat; when steam begins to rise thickly through the holes, add one quarter of the couscous, rubbing it gently between your palms and letting it mound in the center. Reduce heat to moderately high and steam, uncovered, for 5 minutes. Add the remaining couscous, again dribbling it in between your palms, and steam, uncovered, for 20 minutes.

Return couscous to the baking dish. Sprinkle with ½ teaspoon salt and slowly drizzle with ¾ cup cold water. As soon as couscous is cool enough to handle, oil your hands lightly and begin rubbing the couscous between your palms as before to break up any lumps. Set aside at least 10 minutes or up to several hours. Cover lightly with a damp cloth if it will be sitting for more than half an hour.

For final steaming of couscous, steam as before over simmering water for 15 minutes, sealing the rim of the *couscousière* with dampened and floured cheesecloth. (You can reuse the same piece of cheesecloth; just dampen it again.) If indicated in the recipe (as in Couscous with Chicken Wings, page 50), this second steaming should be done over a simmering stew rather than water.

Transfer couscous to a warm bowl and stir in butter with a fork. Taste and add salt if needed.

Makes about 3 cups.

1½ cups couscous
Water
½ tsp. salt
1 Tb. unsalted butter

BUYER'S NOTE

Many supermarkets carry packaged couscous in boxes. Check Middle Eastern stores and natural-food stores for couscous in bulk. It is available in several sizes, from fine-grained to coarse; the various sizes may be used interchangeably. Avoid instant couscous; it has been precooked and gives inferior results.

Quick Couscous

A lthough not as light and fluffy as couscous steamed in a cous-cousière, Quick Couscous is suitable for soups and for "near-soups" like Cuscussu Trapanese (see page 49). When time is short, it's an acceptable substitute in any couscous recipe.

1½ cups water or
   chicken stock (see
   COOK'S NOTE,
   page 14)
½ teaspoon salt (or less
   if chicken stock is
   salted)
1½ cups couscous
3 Tb. unsalted butter, in
   small pieces

Bring water or stock and salt to a boil in a medium saucepan. Add couscous, cover and remove from heat. Let stand 5 minutes. Add butter; fluff with a fork.

If you have a coarse-mesh sieve, you can make an even lighter couscous by passing the grains once through the sieve into another bowl after they've been buttered and fluffed. The sieving breaks up any lumps.

Makes about 3 cups.

Couscous Cream of Wheat

I f you think of cream of wheat as bland, boring nursery food, try making it with toasted couscous. Toasting brings out the grain's nutty flavor, yielding a cereal with far more character than store-bought cream of wheat. Start winter mornings with toasty Couscous Cream of Wheat, adding butter, cream and sugar as your diet allows.

1 cup couscous
1½ cups milk
1 cup water
¼ to ½ tsp. salt
1½ Tb. unsalted butter

Put couscous in a heavy saucepan and set over moderate heat. Toast, shaking pan often, until couscous begins to color, about 5 minutes. Add milk, water and salt to taste. Bring to a simmer, then reduce heat to low and cook, stirring constantly, until mixture is thick and creamy, about 5 minutes. Stir in butter and remove from heat. Serve immediately, with additional butter, cream and sugar or maple syrup.

Makes 3 large or 4 small servings, about 2½ cups total.

Moroccan-Style Chicken Soup

Use the Moroccan spice paste called Harissa to give a kick to your chicken broth, then ladle the broth over couscous and a poached egg. With the ingredients on hand, that's a 15-minute dinner; serve a spinach salad first or roasted bell peppers with lemon and oil.

To make Harissa, combine ingredients in a small bowl. Stir with a fork to blend. Set aside for 1 hour to develop flavors.

Heat chicken stock in a large saucepan over medium heat. Bring to a simmer, then reduce heat to maintain a bare flutter on the surface of the stock. Break eggs one at a time into a small bowl, then carefully slide the eggs into the stock. Poach gently until whites are firm but yolks are still soft, about 3 minutes.

Put ¾ cup cooked couscous into each of four warm soup bowls. Using a slotted spoon, put one poached egg into each bowl atop the couscous. Put a teaspoon of Harissa atop each egg, then divide the hot chicken broth among the four bowls. The Harissa will disperse and the egg will continue cooking slightly in the hot broth. Serve immediately.

Makes 4 servings.

HARISSA
1 tsp. cayenne pepper
1 tsp. hot paprika (see COOK'S NOTE)
1 clove garlic, finely minced
2 tsp. lemon juice
2 tsp. olive oil
Pinch salt

6 cups chicken stock (see COOK'S NOTE, page 14)
4 eggs
1 recipe Quick Couscous (see page 46)

COOK'S NOTE

Most supermarkets carry paprika in both hot and sweet (mild) varieties.

Couscous with Curry Butter, Pistachios and Currants

*A*lthough we encounter couscous mainly in North African food, the grain holds plenty of possibilities for the Western cook. Why not use couscous as a rice substitute—in a pilaf, for example, to accompany lamb chops or kebabs?

½ cup shelled pistachios
1 recipe Basic Couscous
  (see page 44)
6 Tb. currants
3 Tb. unsalted butter
1 cup chopped onion
¾ tsp. curry powder
Salt

Preheat oven to 350°F.

Blanch pistachios 30 seconds in boiling water. Drain and wrap in a clean dishtowel for 3 minutes to "steam" the outer skins loose. Unwrap and remove as much of the skin as possible by rubbing nuts between your fingers. Put them on a baking sheet and toast in the preheated oven until crisp and very lightly browned, about 5 minutes. Set aside to cool. When cool, chop coarsely.

Make Basic Couscous up to final steaming. Stir in currants with a fork and proceed with final steaming.

Melt butter in a skillet over moderate heat. Add onions and curry powder and cook, stirring, until onions are softened, about 5 minutes. Set aside.

Transfer couscous to a warm bowl. Stir in sautéed onions and pistachios with a fork. Toss lightly but well to blend. Season to taste with salt. Serve immediately.

Makes 4 servings.

Cuscussu Trapanese
Sicilian Fish Couscous

Couscous is a North African dish, with one remarkable exception: the cuscussu of Trapani, a town on Sicily's western coast. It's a spicy, fish-based couscous reputedly found nowhere else, although Italophile chef Joyce Goldstein of San Francisco's Square One restaurant makes a venerable version. The rendition below is a hybrid, with the requisite couscous, saffron and harissa, but with an added, delectable dollop of aioli.

To make Fish Stock, put fish bones, water and wine in a heavy saucepan. Bring to a boil slowly, skimming any scum that rises to the surface. When stock boils, add remaining stock ingredients. Return to a boil, then reduce heat to maintain a bare simmer and cook 30 minutes. Strain and set aside.

To make Aioli, whisk egg yolk and warm water together in a small bowl. Begin adding oil drop by drop, whisking constantly as for mayonnaise. When mixture emulsifies, you may add the oil faster, still whisking constantly. Put garlic and salt in a mortar and crush to a paste, or mince garlic and salt to a paste by hand. Add to mayonnaise along with lemon juice. Set aside.

In a large soup pot, heat oil over moderate heat. Add onion and sauté until softened, about 10 minutes. Add saffron and tomatoes and simmer 3 minutes, stirring. Add strained fish stock and simmer until liquid is reduced to about 5 cups. Add salt to taste.

Add fish fillets to stock and simmer gently until just done, about 5 minutes. Divide couscous among four warm soup bowls. Put a fish fillet atop couscous in each bowl. Stir Harissa (to taste) into fish stock, then ladle stock over fish and couscous. Top each portion with a generous dollop of Aioli. Garnish with minced parsley and serve immediately.

Makes 4 servings.

FISH STOCK
2 pounds meaty fish bones
5 cups water
1 cup dry white wine
1 large carrot, coarsely chopped
1 onion, coarsely chopped
2 ribs celery, coarsely chopped
2 sprigs fresh thyme
Several sprigs fresh parsley
1 bay leaf
1 thick slice lemon

AIOLI
1 egg yolk
½ tsp. warm water
⅔ cup olive oil
1 large clove garlic
¼ tsp. salt
½ tsp. lemon juice

1 Tb. olive oil
¾ cup minced onion
About ½ tsp. saffron threads
¾ cup peeled, seeded and diced tomatoes, fresh or canned
Salt
4 firm-fleshed white fish fillets, such as halibut or snapper, about 4 ounces each
1 recipe Quick Couscous (see page 46)
1 recipe Harissa (see page 47)
Minced parsley

Couscous with Chicken Wings

*T*his colorful couscous is a meal in itself. Follow it with orange slices sprinkled with rosewater, small portions of store-bought *baklava and a fragrant hot tea.*

6 chicken wings
Salt
3 Tb. unsalted butter
1 large onion, sliced
Freshly ground black
  pepper
½ tsp. saffron threads
½ tsp. ground ginger
¼ tsp. cayenne pepper
1 Tb. honey
½ cup raisins
½ pound peeled and
  seeded sugar
  pumpkin or other
  small, sweet pumpkin
  or winter squash, in
  ¾-inch cubes
½ pound zucchini, in ¾-
  inch cubes
15-ounce can (1½ cups)
  chick-peas, rinsed
  and drained
1 recipe Basic Couscous
  (see page 44),
  prepared up to final
  steaming
¼ tsp. cinnamon
2 Tb. minced parsley
  mixed with ½ tsp.
  grated lemon rind
Harissa (see page 47)

Cut off wing tips and discard or save for stock. Cut wings in half at joint. Pat dry, then salt well.

In a large Dutch oven or stew pot, melt 2 tablespoons butter over moderate heat. Add chicken wings, outside down, then scatter the sliced onion around them. Add several grinds of black pepper, the saffron, ginger and cayenne pepper. Cover and stew gently for 5 minutes. Turn chicken wings over, cover and stew an additional 5 minutes. Add 2 cups water, bring to a simmer, then reduce heat to low, cover and cook until wings are very tender, about 20 to 30 minutes.

Preheat broiler. Remove wings from stew pot with tongs, letting the juices drip back into the pot. Put the wings on a plate and set aside to cool slightly. Rub wings all over with honey, put them on a rack in a roasting pan and set it in the oven 3 to 4 inches from broiling element. Broil until skin crackles and browns, about 3 minutes. Set wings aside.

Transfer stewing juices in pot to bottom of a dry *couscousière*. Add raisins, pumpkin, zucchini and chick-peas. Bring to a boil over moderately high heat. Set top of *couscousière* over the stew and seal with cheesecloth as directed in the Basic Couscous recipe. When steam begins to rise through top of *couscousière*, slowly dribble couscous in, rubbing it between your palms. Steam 15 minutes, uncovered. Stir cinnamon and remaining tablespoon butter into couscous and toss gently with a fork to blend. Taste and add salt if needed.

Mound couscous on a serving platter and make a well in the center. Place chicken wings in the well. Using a slotted spoon, lift raisins and vegetables out of broth in bottom of *couscousière* and arrange atop the couscous. Spoon a little broth over all. Garnish with parsley-lemon mixture. Pass Harissa and remaining broth separately.

Makes 4 servings.

Couscous with Spicy Lamb "Sausages" and Yogurt Sauce

Moroccan *kefta are highly-spiced lamb patties, formed around skewers and grilled over coals. Serve the lamb on a bed of couscous, the better to trap its peppery juices, and offer a cool yogurt sauce to mute the heat. For a delicious summer dinner, start with a salad of tomatoes, sweet onions and mint and finish with fresh peaches or peach ice cream. Be sure your cayenne pepper and cumin smell fresh and lively before you use them.*

To make Yogurt Sauce, combine yogurt, garlic, scallions and parsley in a small bowl. Whisk well. Season to taste with salt and pepper. Let rest one hour before using; adjust seasoning just before serving.

In a large bowl, combine lamb, bread crumbs, buttermilk, garlic, onion, mint, ½ tsp. cayenne, cumin and black pepper. Refrigerate 1 hour. Add salt, fry a little of the mixture in a skillet, then taste and adjust seasoning.

Form lamb mixture into eight cigar-shaped "sausages" and put two on each of four skewers. Be sure to shape them tightly around the skewer so that they won't fall off or roll around. Brush kebabs lightly with olive oil.

Prepare a medium-hot charcoal fire. When the coals are gray, arrange them in a ring around the perimeter of the grill. Nestle a drip pan made of aluminum foil in the middle.

Oil the grate to keep kebabs from sticking. Arrange kebabs over drip pan and grill, turning occasionally, until well-browned but still juicy within, about 8 minutes.

Put a mound of couscous on each of four warm serving plates; divide skewers among the plates, setting them atop the couscous. Put a dollop of sauce on each "sausage" and pass remaining sauce separately.

Makes 4 servings.

YOGURT SAUCE
1 cup whole-milk yogurt
1 small clove garlic, minced
2 scallions, white part only, minced
2 Tb. minced parsley
Salt and freshly ground black pepper

1 pound freshly ground lamb, from the breast, neck and/or shoulder
¾ cup soft fresh bread crumbs
2 Tb. buttermilk
3 large cloves garlic, minced
½ large onion, very finely chopped
1 Tb. finely chopped fresh mint
1 tsp. cayenne pepper
1½ tsp. ground cumin
Freshly ground black pepper
Salt
Olive oil
1 recipe Basic Couscous (see page 44)

Couscous with Greek-Style Lamb Shanks

I had a Greek roommate in college who made a beef stew unlike any I'd ever tasted. I'd thought cinnamon and cloves were for pies, but Cathy proved otherwise. Only later, when I traveled to Greece, did I realize how traditional her exotic stew was.

Lamb shanks are superb for this treatment, as braising turns them fork-tender and draws their own gelatinous richness into the sauce. Instead of the traditional Greek accompaniment—potatoes, rice or rice-shaped orzo—serve the stew on a mound of fluffy couscous.

4 lamb shanks
1 Tb. unsalted butter
1 Tb. olive oil
Salt and freshly ground
  black pepper
1 large onion, sliced
3 cloves garlic, minced
¼ tsp. ground cloves
2 cups peeled, seeded
  and diced tomato
2 Tb. tomato paste
1 cup red wine
¼ cup red wine vinegar
¾ cup water
1 cinnamon stick, about
  2½ inches long
1 recipe Basic Couscous
  (see page 44)
Minced parsley,
  optional

Have butcher saw lamb shanks in thirds. Melt butter with oil in a large skillet over moderately high heat. Add lamb shanks and brown well on all sides. Season with salt and pepper, then transfer to a large ovenproof baking dish with a lid.

Preheat oven to 325°F.

Pour off all but a tablespoon fat in the skillet. Add onion, garlic and cloves to skillet and sauté until onions are softened and garlic is fragrant, about 5 minutes. Add tomatoes, tomato paste, wine, vinegar, water and cinnamon stick. Bring to a simmer and simmer 5 minutes. Pour over lamb shanks. Cover and bake in the preheated oven until very tender, about 2 hours.

Transfer lamb shanks to a warm platter with a slotted spoon. Cover with foil to keep warm. Pour sauce into a large measuring cup, remove cinnamon stick and let sauce settle 5 minutes. Spoon off any fat that rises to the top. Pour sauce into a skillet and reduce over high heat until slightly thickened.

Mound couscous on a large warm serving platter. Top with lamb shanks and spoon sauce over all. Garnish with minced parsley, if desired.

Makes 4 servings.

Couscous with Coconut, Almonds and Apricots

Serve this couscous as dessert after roast saffron chicken and stewed peppers or grilled lamb chops and baked eggplant. It also makes a delicious breakfast, served with milk or cream. The recipe is flexible: substitute prunes or dates for apricots, walnuts or pistachios for almonds if you prefer.

Toast coconut in a small skillet over low heat, stirring constantly, until lightly and evenly browned. Set aside.

Put apricots in a steamer over boiling water and steam until slightly softened, about 5 minutes. Chop coarsely and set aside.

Bring 1 cup water and the salt to a boil in a small saucepan. Add couscous, cover and remove from heat. Let stand 5 minutes. Stir in 1 tablespoon butter with a fork. Add chopped apricots and toss gently to blend. Transfer mixture to a lightly buttered baking dish that will fit inside your steamer. (Couscous may be prepared ahead up to this point, covered and set aside for up to 2 hours.)

Ten minutes before serving, set couscous dish inside steamer, cover and steam over boiling water 10 minutes or until hot throughout. Remove dish from steamer, add remaining tablespoon butter, half the coconut, all the almonds and half the Cinnamon Sugar. Toss gently with a fork until butter melts. Transfer to a warm serving bowl. Garnish top with remaining coconut and Cinnamon Sugar.

Makes six ½-cup servings.

¼ cup sweetened coconut
10 dried apricots
½ tsp. salt
1 cup couscous
2 Tb. unsalted butter, softened
⅓ cup coarsely chopped toasted almonds
Cinnamon Sugar: 2 tablespoons sugar mixed with ½ teaspoon cinnamon

Cracked Wheat

Cracked Wheat

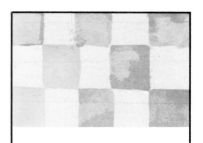

Made from whole, unprocessed wheat berries cracked with steel blades, cracked wheat has all the nutritional advantages of the whole wheat berry.

Although the names are sometimes used interchangeably, bulgur and cracked wheat are slightly different. To make bulgur, the wheat berries are cooked first, then parched to dryness, then cracked—traitionally, by hand with a mortar and pestle; today, in commercial mills. Bulgur has a deeper gold color and a toastier flavor than cracked wheat. Despite its pre-cooking, it can be used interchangeably with cracked wheat in recipes.

Cracked wheat is most closely associated with Middle Eastern cooking, where it is used in such ancient dishes as tabbouleh (a cracked wheat and raw vegetable salad) and kibbe (cracked wheat pounded to a paste with raw lamb).

Like so many grains, it makes a delicious breakfast cereal, especially when simmered with dates and cream (page 59). Add cooked cracked wheat to a whole wheat and walnut bread (page 60) for extra nutrition and texture. Combine it with couscous and scallions to make a two-grain pilaf (page 63) that could partner just about anything.

A SPRING PICNIC

After a winter of San Francisco rain, I can hardly wait for the day that's pretty enough to picnic. The following menu can be packed to travel. Put the hot soup in a thermos that you've warmed first with boiling water. The pita toasts can go in an airtight cookie tin, the salad in a plastic container. To do without plates entirely, take some hearts of romaine to scoop up the cracked wheat salad.

Roasted Eggplant Soup

Herbed Pita Toasts

Cracked Wheat Salad with Zucchini and Mint (page 61)

Fresh Cherries and Apricots

Basic Cracked Wheat

Cracked wheat can be cooked by a variety of different methods, depending on what you intend to do with the finished product. For salads, you want a firm texture with some "tooth" to it; for breakfast cereal, you want a soft porridge; for a hot side dish or pilaf, you want a light and fluffy texture.

For cracked wheat to be used in salads, cover 1 part cracked wheat with 2 parts boiling water. Let stand, uncovered, 10 to 15 minutes, then drain in a colander. Squeeze cracked wheat dry in a double thickness of cheesecloth. Transfer to a bowl and fluff with a fork (see Cracked Wheat Salad with Zucchini, Lemon and Mint, page 61).

For cracked wheat as breakfast cereal, cook 1 part cracked wheat in 4 parts simmering water, stirring often, for about 20 minutes or until it is as soft as you like. Add butter, spices, nuts, fruits, milk or cream, honey or sugar (see Cracked Wheat Porridge with Dates and Cream, page 59).

For cracked wheat as a pilaf, toast cracked wheat briefly in butter, then add 2 parts hot liquid to 1 part wheat. Cover and cook over low heat for 15 minutes. Set aside and let stand 5 minutes, then fluff with a fork (see Cracked Wheat and Couscous Pilaf, page 63).

BUYER'S NOTE

Look for cracked wheat or bulgur in bulk or in packages at natural-food stores, Middle Eastern markets and well-stocked supermarkets. Some stores carry fine, medium and coarse sizes. The recipes that follow were tested with medium cracked wheat; if using fine or coarse cracked wheat, you may have to adjust cooking times slightly.

Cracked Wheat Porridge
with Dates and Cream

Cracked wheat becomes thick and creamy when it's cooked and stirred in plenty of water. Add a nugget of sweet butter, a drizzle of cream and a handful of moist chopped dates for the sort of breakfast you can scale mountains on. No need to add sugar—the dates provide plenty of natural sweetness.

The plump Medjool dates are the best. When my neighborhood produce market started placing them at the checkout counter in an invitingly open box, my grocery bill started mounting. I can't resist these lovely dates. One or two after dinner with a cup of tea satisfies my sweet tooth, and I was delighted to discover what they do for breakfast porridge.

Bring lightly salted water to boil in a saucepan. Add cracked wheat and cook over medium heat, stirring often, until water has been absorbed and porridge thickens, about 20 minutes. Stir in chopped dates. Divide porridge among four warm bowls. Top each serving with one teaspoon butter and a tablespoon of heavy cream.

Makes 4 servings.

4 cups water
Salt
1 cup cracked wheat
10 Medjool dates, pitted
    and coarsely chopped
4 tsp. unsalted butter
4 Tb. heavy cream

Cracked Wheat and Walnut Bread

A dense, moist loaf loaded with toasted walnuts, this bread is a great choice to accompany a cheese platter. If you're picnicking, use it for cream cheese-and-watercress sandwiches or for bread-and-butter sandwiches with a cold roast chicken. The bread is best sliced thin.

⅓ cup cracked wheat
1 package dry yeast
⅓ cup warm water
  (105°F. to 110°F.)
Pinch sugar
1 cup milk
4 Tb. unsalted butter
2 tsp. salt
¼ cup walnut oil
½ cup walnuts, toasted
  and ground
¾ cup walnuts, toasted
  and coarsely chopped
1½ cups whole wheat
  flour
About 2½ cups all-
  purpose unbleached
  flour
2 Tb. cornmeal

Cover cracked wheat with 1 cup boiling water and let stand 1 hour. Drain thoroughly and set aside.

Dissolve yeast in the warm water with the sugar. Let stand until foamy.

Heat milk, butter and salt slowly until butter melts. Let cool to about 110°F.

In a large bowl, combine proofed yeast, milk mixture, walnut oil, ground walnuts, chopped walnuts and cracked wheat and stir until smooth. Add whole wheat flour and beat about 2 minutes. Beat in remaining flour, a little at a time. When dough becomes too stiff to stir, turn out onto a lightly floured board. Knead about 10 minutes, adding more flour as necessary to make a stiff, smooth dough. Form dough into a ball, transfer to a clean, buttered bowl and turn to coat all sides with butter. Cover bowl tightly with plastic wrap and let rise until double, about 1½ hours. Punch dough down and knead briefly. Shape into a ball and place on a heavy baking sheet sprinkled with cornmeal. Cover loosely with a towel and let rise until double, about 1 hour.

Preheat oven to 425°F.

Slash dough on top with scissors or a sharp knife. Put a pan of hot water or several ice cubes on the oven floor to create steam. Bake bread 30 minutes, then reduce heat to 375°F. and bake until bread is well-browned and sounds hollow when tapped on the bottom, about 30 minutes more. Cool completely on a rack before slicing.

Makes one 2½-pound loaf.

Cracked Wheat Salad
with Zucchini, Lemon and Mint

A variation on Middle Eastern tabbouleh, this cool cracked wheat salad makes a refreshing summer first course or an appealing partner for cold lamb. Instead of the feta, you could spoon some creamy yogurt on top. I discovered this great combination in the lunchroom at Ratto's, an international market in Oakland, California. Mrs. Durante, the proprietor's wife, makes her own yogurt for the tabbouleh.

The salad's textures and flavors are at their best shortly after it's made. If you need to make it ahead, adjust the seasonings just before serving. It will probably need another squeeze of lemon. Cooked and cooled wild rice could be substituted for the cracked wheat, if desired.

Cover cracked wheat with 4 cups boiling water and soak for 30 minutes. Drain thoroughly and cool. Squeeze cracked wheat dry in a double thickness of cheesecloth. Transfer grains to a bowl and fluff with a fork. Add zucchini, radishes, scallions, garlic, parsley and mint and toss to blend. Add lemon juice, olive oil and salt and pepper to taste. If using feta, stir in with a fork.

Makes 6 servings.

2 cups cracked wheat
2 small zucchini, coarsely grated
12 radishes, thinly sliced
½ cup minced scallions
1 clove garlic, minced
¼ cup minced parsley
2 Tb. finely chopped fresh mint
¼ cup lemon juice
¼ cup olive oil
Salt and pepper
5 ounces crumbled feta cheese, optional

Lebanese Lamb Tartare

*T*he traditional Middle Eastern kibbe *is made of lamb, cracked wheat and spices massaged to a paste. But the dish is as good, if not better, when all the textures are distinct, and when it's prepared at the last minute like a steak tartare. Mound it on a platter or on individual serving plates, surround it with hearts of romaine lettuce and toasted wedges of pita bread and serve it with sparkling wine as an appetizer.*

½ cup cracked wheat
½ tsp. cuminseed
1 pound lean boneless leg of lamb, trimmed of all fat and connective tissue
6 scallions, minced
2 Tb. minced cilantro or mint
2 Tb. minced parsley
¼ cup pine nuts, toasted
2 cloves garlic, minced
¼ tsp. cayenne pepper
¼ cup lemon juice
2 Tb. olive oil
Salt and freshly ground black pepper
Additional olive oil and cayenne pepper, for garnish
Hearts of romaine and toasted pita bread, for serving

Put cracked wheat in a small bowl and cover with 1 cup boiling water. Let soak 20 minutes, then drain and squeeze dry in a double thickness of cheesecloth. Transfer to a small bowl and fluff with a fork to separate the grains.

Toast cuminseed in a small skillet over moderate heat until it is fragrant but not smoking. Grind to a powder with a mortar and pestle or an electric spice grinder.

Put meat through medium blade of a meat grinder. Transfer to a bowl and add cracked wheat, cumin, scallions, cilantro or mint, parsley, pine nuts, garlic, cayenne, lemon juice and olive oil. Blend quickly and lightly with your fingertips. Season to taste with salt and pepper and add more lemon or spices to taste. The mixture should be spicy and lemony.

Divide the lamb into eight portions and mound each on a small salad plate. Spoon two teaspoons olive oil over each serving and sprinkle each with cayenne. Or, mound the entire mixture on a large serving platter, drizzle ⅓ cup olive oil over it and sprinkle with cayenne. Serve with hearts of romaine and toasted wedges of pita bread.

Makes 8 servings.

Cracked Wheat and Couscous Pilaf

A pilaf as simple as this one points up the natural good flavor of grains and reminds us how underutilized they are in the American kitchen. Cook the cracked wheat and couscous separately, then combine them at the last minute for a couldn't-be-easier side dish for meats and poultry. Serve it with a beef brisket or a bronzed roast duck, or add herbs or spices and use it as a poultry stuffing.

Melt 1 tablespoon butter and the oil in a heavy saucepan over moderately high heat. Add scallions and cracked wheat and cook, stirring, until scallions are fragrant and wheat is lightly toasted. Add 2 cups chicken stock, cover, reduce heat to low and simmer 15 minutes. Set aside, covered, 5 minutes.

Bring remaining cup chicken stock to a boil in a small saucepan. Add couscous, cover and remove from heat. Let stand 5 minutes, then stir in remaining tablespoon butter with a fork.

Combine cracked wheat and couscous, mixing and fluffing them gently with a fork to blend. Season to taste with salt and pepper. Transfer to a warm serving bowl.

Makes 6 to 8 servings, 6 cups total.

2 Tb. unsalted butter
1 Tb. olive oil
6 scallions, thinly sliced
1 cup cracked wheat
3 cups hot chicken stock (see COOK'S NOTE, page 14)
1 cup couscous
Salt and freshly ground black pepper

Hominy

Hominy

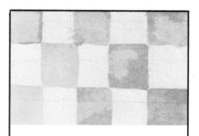

When the first English settlers arrived in Virginia in 1607, they found Indians eating foods they'd never seen before. One of these was "rockahominie," the Indian word for dried white field corn. The settlers were taught to soak the corn in a wood ash solution to loosen the outer husk, then to cook it in clean, fresh water until it was tender. They shortened the name to "hominy," and the dish became a staple in their diet.

Ground fine, the dried corn is called hominy grits—or just grits—and it's on the breakfast plate at diners from Baltimore to Baton Rouge. At their worst, hominy grits are thin, watery and bland. At their best, they're soft and fluffy, with a distinct corn flavor. Like corn on the cob, grits are made to be slathered with butter.

Use whole hominy in Mexican-style soups, simmer it in cream, scramble it with eggs and sausage, or braise it with meaty pork riblets and chorizo. Grits make delicious baked puddings and soufflés, especially when given a lift with garlic, cheese, herbs and/or chilies.

A PATIO PARTY

This menu suggests to me a midsummer patio party, with mariachi music, piñatas and bright paper flowers. You could have a variety of Mexican beers iced down in washtubs or big pitchers of iced red and white sangria. The pig should be carved into small pieces after grilling so that guests can make their own tacos with guacamole.

Cocktail Quesadillas

Spit-roasted Suckling Pig with Mexican Spice Rub

Guacamole

Tomato and Hominy Salad with Cilantro and Lime (page 73)

Hot Tortillas

Tequila-plugged Melons

Basic Hominy

Making hominy from dried corn has to be one of the most tedious procedures in cooking. There is no question that hominy prepared from scratch has more corn flavor than canned, but unless you have a trained staff of monkeys, you won't want to do it. Directions are given below for the determined. You may want to try it once, just to taste the difference. The method is adapted from the one recommended by cookbook author Diana Kennedy.

Canned hominy, well-rinsed, was used for all the recipes in this book and found delicious.

2 cups dried white or yellow corn

½ tsp. slaked lime (calcium hydroxide, see Buyer's Note)

Put dried corn in a large saucepan and cover with cold water. Cover pan and soak corn overnight. Drain and return corn to saucepan with fresh water. Bring to a boil and add lime, stirring well. Boil 10 minutes, then cover and set aside for 30 minutes. Rinse corn very well under cold running water, rubbing it between your fingers to remove any loosened papery outer skin.

Use your fingertips to pinch off the dark germ at the base of each kernel. Pull the papery skin off along with it. Rinse kernels again and put in a saucepan with 8 cups water. Bring to a boil, reduce heat to maintain a simmer, cover and cook until tender, 1 to 1½ hours. (If you will be cooking the hominy further in soups or stews, undercook it slightly.) Drain and use as desired.

Makes about 5 cups.

BUYER'S NOTE

Canned, fully-cooked whole hominy is available in most supermarkets in both white and golden varieties; they are interchangeable. Quick-cooking grits and instant grits (see page 69) are also available in many supermarkets nationwide. For regular grits, you may have to write to a friend or relative south of the Mason-Dixon line. Latin markets and tortilla factories are the best source for dried whole corn and the slaked lime (calcium hydroxide) needed for soaking.

Basic Grits

A Southern breakfast staple, usually served with a puddle of butter or meat gravy.

Bring water and salt to a boil in a saucepan. Add grits in a slow stream, whisking constantly. Reduce heat to low, cover and cook until smooth and thick, stirring occasionally, about 15 to 20 minutes. Set aside 5 minutes, covered, then stir in butter to taste.

Serve with milk and sugar or maple syrup for breakfast, or add freshly ground black pepper and more salt for a dinner side dish.

Makes 4 servings.

4 cups water
Pinch salt
1 cup regular grits
Butter

ABOUT QUICK-COOKING GRITS

Quick-cooking grits have been cracked finer than regular grits, so they take only 6 or 7 minutes to cook. I find next-to-no difference between quick-cooking and regular grits. Prepare quick-cooking grits according to package directions.

ABOUT INSTANT GRITS

Instant grits have been precooked and dehydrated. Boiling water rehydrates them immediately. Prepare them according to package directions. Instant grits should not be substituted for quick grits in the recipes that follow.

Garlic Cheddar Grits

*S*oft and creamy like Southern spoonbread, these grits are *fragrant with garlic and cheese. Serve with sliced ripe to-matoes for a summer brunch or a Sunday supper; or serve as a side dish with grilled sausage or chicken.*

2 cups milk
1 cup chicken stock
(see COOK'S NOTE, page 14)
¾ cup quick (not "instant") grits
3 Tb. unsalted butter
1 cup grated Cheddar cheese
2 cloves garlic, minced
Salt and freshly ground black pepper
3 eggs, lightly beaten

Preheat oven to 350°F.

Combine milk and chicken stock in a heavy saucepan and bring to a simmer over moderate heat. Add grits in a slow stream, whisking constantly. Reduce heat to low and cook, whisking constantly, until mixture is thick and smooth, 6 to 7 minutes. Whisk in butter, ¾ cup Cheddar and garlic. Season to taste with salt and pepper. Remove from heat and whisk in eggs.

Pour batter into a well-buttered 1½-quart baking dish and bake until firm to the touch and lightly browned on top, about 30 minutes. Sprinkle remaining Cheddar on top and return to the oven for 5 minutes. Serve immediately.

Makes 4 servings.

VARIATION

Add one 4-ounce can chopped green chilies (well-drained) along with the butter, cheese and garlic.

Souffléed Grits and Chives

*W*ith the addition of beaten egg whites, cooked grits become *an airy soufflé. The spoon that breaks its golden crust releases the lively aroma of fresh chives.*

Combine milk and water in a saucepan and bring to a simmer. Add grits in a slow, steady stream, whisking constantly. Reduce heat to low and cook, whisking often, until grits are thick and creamy, about 7 minutes. Remove from heat and stir in butter. Add egg yolks one at a time, whisking well after each addition. Stir in chives. Add salt and pepper. Let cool slightly.

Preheat oven to 400°F. Butter a 2-quart soufflé dish and dust the sides with the bread crumbs, shaking out excess.

Beat egg whites to firm peaks, then fold them gently into the soufflé base. Pour the batter into prepared soufflé dish and bake until puffed and lightly browned, 25 to 30 minutes.

Makes 4 servings.

1 cup milk
1 cup water
½ cup quick (not "instant") grits
2 Tb. unsalted butter
3 eggs, separated
½ cup minced fresh chives
½ tsp. coarse salt
Freshly ground black pepper
Fine bread crumbs

Hominy in Cream

*H*ere's a simple but rich side dish to have with pork chops or pan-fried sausage. With bacon or sausage and stewed fruit, it makes a fine breakfast, especially if you'll be sawing logs or skiing all morning.

2 cups cooked whole hominy (if canned, rinse and drain well)
⅔ cup heavy cream
2 Tb. unsalted butter
Salt and freshly ground black pepper

Simmer hominy, cream and butter in a saucepan until cream is reduced and thickened, about 2 minutes. Add salt and pepper to taste and serve hot.

Makes 4 servings.

Hominy, Chorizo and Eggs

*H*ome economists are constantly developing good recipes for the back of food packages and labels. They hope to hook you on the recipe so you'll use the product again and again. The recipe below is a variation of one I found on a can of hominy. Served with a pile of hot corn tortillas, it makes a wonderful brunch or supper dish.

¼ pound chorizo or linguiça sausage
2 Tb. olive oil
1 Tb. unsalted butter
½ onion, minced
1 cup cooked whole hominy
4 eggs
2 Tb. heavy cream
Salt and freshly ground black pepper
Minced chives, parsley or cilantro

Remove casings from sausage. Heat 1 tablespoon oil in a small skillet over moderately low heat. Crumble sausage coarsely, add to skillet and cook until hot throughout. Drain sausage in a sieve.

Heat remaining oil and butter in a clean skillet over moderately low heat. Add onion and sauté until softened, about 5 minutes. Add hominy and cook until hot throughout. Beat eggs and cream together lightly, then add to skillet. Reduce heat to low and cook, stirring often, until eggs are just barely set.

Season lightly with salt and pepper (chorizo is spicy) and stir in minced herbs. Just before serving, gently stir in chorizo. Divide between two warm plates. Serve immediately.

Makes 2 to 3 servings.

Tomato and Hominy Salad
with Cilantro and Lime

*T*his colorful summer salad would flatter barbecued foods and would be tempting on a summer buffet. You can prepare the parts ahead, but assemble it just before serving.

In a large bowl, combine all ingredients except salt and pepper. Toss together lightly, then add salt and pepper to taste. Serve immediately.

    Makes 4 servings.

2 cups cooked whole hominy

2 cups peeled, seeded and diced ripe tomato

½ cup minced red onion

½ cup minced green bell pepper

½ jalapeño pepper, minced (with seeds)

3 Tb. minced cilantro

3 Tb. lime juice

1 Tb. minced garlic

2 Tb. extra-virgin olive oil

Salt and freshly ground black pepper

California Succotash

The native Americans made their succotash with corn and kidney beans in bear fat, but modern renditions lean to corn, limas and salt pork. For an agreeable winter version, substitute hominy for fresh corn, and add a little minced red pepper for color and sweetness. Season well with black pepper and serve with pork, grilled chicken or fried rabbit.

6 slices bacon, cut in ¼-inch widths

½ large red bell pepper, seeded and finely diced

1½ cups cooked whole hominy

1½ cups cooked baby lima beans

1 tsp. dried oregano

Salt and freshly ground black pepper

¾ cup thinly sliced scallions

Render bacon in a large heavy skillet over moderate heat. When crisp, transfer to paper towels to drain. Pour off all but 2 tablespoons fat in skillet. Add bell pepper to skillet and sauté over moderately low heat for 10 minutes. Add hominy, lima beans and oregano and sauté until everything is heated through. Season to taste with salt and pepper. Stir in scallions and bacon and transfer to a warm serving bowl.

Makes 4 servings.

Tomato and Hominy Soup

Although made in less than an hour, this soup has a slow-cooked Latin flavor. Serve with warm tortillas for lunch or a light dinner, and offer extra bowls of minced onion and sliced chilies. For a more substantial meal, follow it with pork chops and "a mess o' greens."

Heat oil in a heavy stockpot over moderately low heat. Add onion, garlic, jalapeño and oregano and sauté until onions are softened, about 10 minutes. Add tomato, bring to a simmer, then reduce heat to maintain a slow simmer and cook 20 minutes.

Broil green pepper about six inches from heat until blackened on all sides. Put it in a paper bag and let it steam until cool enough to handle. Peel, remove ribs and seeds and cut into small dice. Stir pepper into stockpot along with chicken stock and hominy. Bring to a simmer over moderately high heat. Reduce heat and simmer slowly for 15 minutes. Season to taste with salt and pepper. Serve immediately.

Makes 3 to 4 servings, about 6 cups total.

1 Tb. peanut oil
1 cup chopped onion
2 cloves garlic, minced
½ jalapeño pepper, minced (with seeds)
1½ tsp. dried oregano
2 cups crushed canned tomato with juices
1 green bell pepper
3 cups chicken stock (see COOK'S NOTE, page 14)
2 cups cooked whole hominy
Salt and freshly ground black pepper

Pork, Chorizo and Hominy Stew

Here's an outrageously good stew prepared with modest expense and attention. Most butchers can supply you with country-style pork ribs, which are meaty ribs cut from the loin. Here, they're braised to fork-tenderness and served in a stew with crumbled chorizo and hominy. It's spicy, stick-to-the-ribs fare for cold weather and big appetites, and like most such stews it's best made a day ahead. Serve with hot tortillas and cold beer.

2½ pounds country-style spareribs

1 pound pork neck bones

1 onion, sliced

3 cloves garlic, peeled and lightly crushed

10 black peppercorns

2 bay leaves

1 pound chorizo sausage

1 onion, minced

2 cloves garlic, minced

½ green bell pepper, seeded and minced

½ jalapeño pepper, minced (with seeds)

1 tsp. dried oregano

1 tsp. ground cumin

1 Tb. flour

3 Tb. minced cilantro

1½ cups cooked whole hominy

Salt and freshly ground black pepper

Put spareribs and neck bones in a large pot with sliced onion, crushed garlic, peppercorns and bay leaves. Add 8 cups water. Bring to a simmer over moderately high heat, skimming any foam that collects on the surface. Reduce heat to maintain a simmer and cook, skimming as necessary, for 40 minutes. Drain, reserving pork and broth separately.

Slit open chorizo casing and crumble chorizo into a large skillet. Cook over moderately low heat, breaking it up with a wooden spoon, until hot throughout. Transfer to a sieve set over a bowl to drain off fat.

Put 3 tablespoons rendered chorizo fat in a clean stockpot and set over moderate heat. Add minced onion and garlic, bell pepper, jalapeño, oregano and cumin and cook, stirring constantly, until onion and pepper are softened, about 10 minutes. Add flour and cook 3 minutes. Add spareribs, cilantro and 5 cups pork broth (save any remaining broth). Bring to a simmer, reduce heat to low and simmer, partially covered, until pork is very tender, about 45 minutes. Add hominy and cook 15 minutes more. Cool and chill.

The next day, lift off any solidified fat and reheat soup, adding a little more broth if necessary. Taste and adjust seasoning, adding salt and pepper as necessary.

Makes 4 servings.

Creamed Hominy Bread

*T*his cream-colored bread has a dense, soft texture; it keeps well and toasts beautifully. It's also a pleasure to make, for the dough is supple and easy to handle.

Bring hominy and 1 cup milk to a simmer in a saucepan over moderately high heat. Reduce heat to maintain a simmer, cover and cook 15 minutes. Stir in sugar, butter and salt and cook, covered, an additional 5 minutes. Transfer to a food processor or blender and puree.

Transfer hominy mixture to a large bowl and stir in remaining ½ cup milk. Mixture should be barely warm. If not, let cool to about 110°F., then stir in yeast. Begin adding flour ½ cup at a time, stirring well after each addition. When mixture is too stiff to stir, turn out on a lightly floured surface. Knead about 10 minutes, adding more flour as necessary to make a firm, smooth, non-sticky dough.

Transfer dough to a buttered bowl and turn to coat all sides with butter. Cover and let rise until double, about 1¼ hours. Punch down and divide dough in half. Shape each half into a loaf and place in a buttered 8-inch loaf pan. Cover and let rise until double, about 1 hour.

Preheat oven to 400°F. Bake loaves until they are well-browned and sound hollow when tapped on the bottom, about 40 minutes.

Makes two 8-inch loaves.

2 cups cooked whole hominy
1½ cups milk
¼ cup sugar
2 Tb. unsalted butter
2 tsp. salt
1 package active dry yeast
About 4 cups all-purpose unbleached flour

millet

Millet

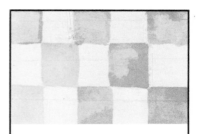

Millet grows well in harsh climates and poor soils, thriving where a wheat or rice crop might fail. It's an important part of the diet in northern India and northern China, especially among peasants who can't afford more expensive grains. The Chinese turn millet into pancakes, breads and porridge; the Indians use it for breads, breakfast cereals and pilaf. In Ethiopia, millet flour is made into the spongy, crepe-like *injera* that is the foundation of an Ethiopian meal.

In this country, most millet goes for birdseed mixtures, although perhaps the grain's high fiber content will lead more consumers to give it a try. It is admittedly bland on its own, but a little butter, salt or sugar turns it into a fine side dish or breakfast. With spices, onions and stock, it becomes an unusual crunchy pilaf to serve with roast poultry, stir-fries or curries. Add cooked millet to bread doughs, meat loaves or stuffings for extra flavor and texture. You can use cooked and seasoned millet to stuff green peppers or baked tomatoes, or you can bake it with eggs, milk and cheese to make a sort of soufflé.

There's nothing sexy about millet. You never see it on restaurant menus or at fancy dinners. Yet I believe it's one of the most adaptable and texturally interesting grains on the shelf. Perhaps if suppliers tripled the price and made it a scarce commodity, we'd see millet becoming the next "gourmet grain." As it is, it's humble fare, but it sure tastes grand. I'm only sorry it took me so many years to discover that!

AN AUTUMN PICNIC

An autumn picnic or tailgate party calls for sturdy food that stands up to travel. Pack hot carrot soup into insulated containers; wrap sandwiches of thin-sliced meat loaf in plastic or foil. At the stadium or picnic site, guests can add cole slaw to their sandwiches if they like.

Carrot Cider Soup

*Millet Meat Loaf
Sandwiches
on Corn Rye
(page 86)*

Buttermilk Cole Slaw

Red and Green Apples

Soft Gingerbread

Basic Millet

S teamed millet seasoned simply with butter, salt and pepper makes a crunchy side dish for grilled or roasted meats and stews. Try it with a stir-fry of pork and sweet peppers, with highly-seasoned lamb kebabs or with a crisp roast duck.

1½ cups water
Pinch salt
1 cup millet
2 Tb. unsalted butter
Freshly ground black
   pepper

Bring water and salt to a boil in a saucepan. Add millet, reduce heat to low, cover and cook 15 minutes. Set aside, covered, 10 minutes. Uncover and stir in butter and plenty of black pepper. Add more salt if desired.

   Makes about 4 cups.

BUYER'S NOTE

Look for millet in natural-food stores and Indian markets. It is generally sold in bulk.

Breakfast Millet with Honey Butter

I f you enjoy something hot and filling in the morning, you should lay in a millet supply. It cooks quickly, and its crunchy texture and nutty flavor are perfect foils for butter and cream. Sweeten it with honey or maple syrup, or add a handful of golden raisins to the simmering water when you stir in the millet.

1½ cups water
Pinch salt
1 cup millet
3 Tb. unsalted butter
1 Tb. honey
Milk or cream, for
   serving

Bring water and salt to a boil in a small saucepan. Add millet, cover and reduce heat to low. Cook 15 minutes. Remove from heat and let stand, covered, 10 minutes.

   Whip butter with honey and stir into millet with a fork. Serve immediately with a pitcher of milk or cream.

   Makes 4 servings.

Millet Maple Bread

Millet adds crunch and fiber to this sturdy breakfast bread; whole wheat and maple syrup lend flavor and a rich brown crust. Cracked wheat may be substituted for the millet, although it should be soaked in the hot water only about 20 minutes to soften it.

Cover millet with boiling water and soak for one hour; drain. Repeat twice with fresh boiling water, soaking one hour each time. Drain well and set millet aside to cool.

Dissolve yeast and sugar in ¼ cup warm water. Bring milk to a simmer in a small saucepan, stirring often to prevent scorching. Transfer milk to a large bowl; add remaining warm water and maple syrup and cool to lukewarm. Stir in yeast mixture and 3 cups whole wheat flour to make a "sponge." Cover bowl with plastic wrap and let sponge rise one hour.

Stir down sponge. Add salt, vegetable oil, millet and remaining whole wheat flour. Add all-purpose flour ½ cup at a time, beating well with a wooden spoon. When dough becomes too stiff to stir, turn out onto a lightly floured board. Knead gently, incorporating more flour as necessary, until dough is smooth and no longer sticky, about 10 minutes. Transfer dough to a clean, well-buttered bowl, turning to coat all sides with butter. Cover bowl tightly with plastic wrap and let dough rise until double, about 2 hours.

Punch dough down, divide in half, and form each half into a loaf. Transfer loaves to well-buttered, 8-inch loaf pans and let rise until almost double, about 1 hour. Preheat oven to 400°F. Brush each loaf with egg wash. Bake in the preheated oven for 30 minutes, then reduce heat to 350°F. and bake until loaves are well-browned and sound hollow when tapped on the bottom, 10 to 15 minutes more. Cool completely on racks before slicing.

Makes 2 loaves.

1 cup millet
1 package dry yeast
Pinch sugar
1½ cups warm water (105°F. to 110°F.)
1½ cups milk
⅓ cup maple syrup
4 cups whole wheat flour
1 Tb. salt
¼ cup vegetable oil
About 2 cups all-purpose unbleached flour
Egg wash: 1 egg beaten with 2 Tb. cream

Fried Millet with Scallions and Eggs

Cold cooked millet has few charms of its own, but it's the start of some fine variations on the fried-rice theme. Toast the grains in butter, then add the seasonings of your choice—minced scallions, diced ham, fresh dill, chopped browned onions—and just enough egg to enrich the dish and bind it lightly. Fried millet on its own is a great Sunday night supper; as a side dish, it could partner a juicy roast duck or chicken, some pan-fried quail or pork chops.

4 Tb. unsalted butter
Basic Millet (page 82), cooled
Salt and freshly ground black pepper
⅓ cup minced scallion
2 eggs, lightly beaten

Melt butter in a large skillet over moderate heat. Add millet and break up any lumps with a fork. Cook, stirring constantly, until millet is hot throughout, 3 to 4 minutes. Season to taste with salt and pepper, then stir in scallion. Remove from heat and stir in eggs.

Makes 4 servings.

Cashew Millet

This simple pilaf is a blueprint for your own variations. Substitute pumpkin seeds for the cashews or mint for cilantro, if you like. To give it more of an Indian flavor—to accompany tandoori-style chicken, for example—you might add some toasted cumin or minced green chilies. If you don't count calories, deep-fry the cashews and sprinkle them while they're hot with coarse salt and chili powder.

Preheat oven to 325°F. Toast cashews on a baking sheet, shaking sheet occasionally, until golden brown, about 10 minutes. Set aside.

Bring water and salt to a boil in a 2-quart saucepan over high heat. Add millet, cover and reduce heat to low. Cook 15 minutes. Remove from heat and let stand, covered, for 10 minutes. Uncover and add butter, scallion, parsley or cilantro, and cashews. Toss gently with a fork until butter melts. Add plenty of black pepper and more salt if necessary. Serve immediately.

Makes 6 servings, about 4 cups total.

⅓ cup raw (unroasted) cashews
1½ cups water
½ tsp. salt
1 cup millet
1½ Tb. unsalted butter, in small pieces
⅓ cup minced scallion
2 Tb. minced parsley or cilantro
Freshly ground black pepper

Millet Meat Loaf

Meat Loaf Lovers of the World (M.E.L.L.O.W.), here's another one for the files. It's highly seasoned, incredibly moist, and even better the following day. Let rest at least 20 minutes after baking to settle the juices. For sandwiches, chill it, slice it thin and serve it on dark, dense bread with a swipe of good mustard.

⅔ pound ground beef

⅔ pound ground veal

⅔ pound sausage meat, mild or spicy

1½ cups cooked millet (see COOK'S NOTE)

2 eggs, lightly beaten

1 cup soft fresh bread crumbs

¼ cup buttermilk

1 large clove garlic, minced

½ cup minced onion

¼ cup minced parsley

1½ tsp. minced fresh oregano

2 tsp. salt

Freshly ground black pepper

3 slices bacon, halved, optional

Preheat oven to 325°F.

Put all ingredients except bacon in a large bowl. Work lightly with your hands just to blend; do not overmix. Fry a little bit of the mixture in an oiled skillet; taste and adjust seasoning. Form mixture into a loaf shape and transfer to a 9-inch loaf pan.

If desired, arrange bacon strips over the top. Bake until internal temperature reaches 150°F, about 1 hour and 10 minutes.

Makes 4 servings.

COOK'S NOTE

A half-recipe Basic Millet (page 82) will yield slightly more than you need for this recipe. Omit butter.

Millet and Ham Hocks

Here's just one more delicious example of how grains can make a little meat go a long way. When cooked with millet, onions and peppers, one ham hock can satisfy four people. After blanching to remove excess salt, the hock is used to make a flavorful stock for steaming the millet. Have sliced tomatoes or a green salad first, and offer beer or a Zinfandel with this simple dish.

Put ham hocks in large kettle and cover with cold water. Bring to a boil, then drain and rinse. If ham tastes salty, blanch and drain again. Return to clean kettle with clove-studded onion and bay leaves. Add 6 cups cold water. Bring slowly to a boil, reduce heat and simmer, uncovered, for 2 hours. Drain, saving liquid and ham hocks, but discarding onion and bay leaves. When hocks are cool enough to handle, remove the meat and chop it coarsely.

In a separate kettle, melt butter over moderate heat. Add minced onion, garlic, bell pepper and cayenne. Sauté, stirring often, until vegetables are softened, about 10 minutes. Add millet and 2¼ cups hot liquid drained from ham hocks. Bring to a boil, cover, reduce heat to low and cook 18 minutes. Uncover, stir in chopped ham with a fork. Season with plenty of black pepper and add salt if necessary.

Makes 4 main-course servings.

1 to 1½ pounds meaty ham hocks (one hock sawed in thirds)
½ onion, studded with 2 cloves
2 bay leaves
3 Tb. unsalted butter
1 cup minced onion
2 small cloves garlic, minced
1 green bell pepper, seeded, deribbed and diced
¼ tsp. cayenne pepper
1½ cups millet
Freshly ground black pepper

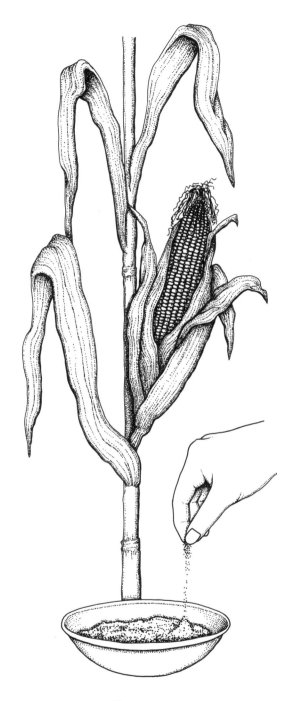

Polenta

Polenta

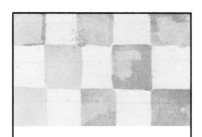

Italians didn't start eating corn until the middle of the seventeenth century, but they quickly made up for lost time. Peasant cooks discovered that coarsely-ground cornmeal made delicious polenta, a sort of porridge that had been made from a variety of grains since Roman times.

Today corn is planted throughout Italy but most heavily in the north. Not only is cornmeal polenta a foundation of humble diets in the mountainous north, often substituting for bread, but it figures prominently on the restaurant menus of Milan and Venice.

What makes polenta so enticing is its versatility. You can serve it while it's hot and creamy, with a puddle of herb butter or butter and maple syrup. Or you can pour it into a buttered mold while it's hot, then unmold it when it cools and firms. You can cool it until it's firm enough to slice, then cut it with decorative cutters or cut it by hand into simple rectangles or diamonds. Cold, day-old polenta can be pan-fried in butter, grilled over coals (be sure to oil the grill) or layered in a buttered casserole with all manner of good things: Gorgonzola or fontina cheese, tomato or mushroom sauce, crumbled sausage, sautéed peppers, fried onions. After layering, the casserole is baked until hot throughout.

SUMMER GRILLED CHICKEN DINNER

In nice weather, you could set a table on your porch or patio for this summer dinner. You won't need to run back and forth to the kitchen as all the cooking can be done ahead. The chicken tastes better if it's not hot off the grill; cook it and set it aside while you sit down to the tomato salad. Even the green beans can be steamed ahead and served at room temperature.

Tomato Salad with Anchovies and Capers

Grilled Chicken with Garlic Mayonnaise

Green Beans

Polenta Country Cake with Fresh Peaches (page 99)

Basic Polenta

You'll never have lumpy polenta if you start stirring with a wire whisk and switch to a wooden spoon only when the mixture thickens. The first version below yields a stiff polenta, a good foundation for saucy dishes like Polenta with Barolo Wine Sauce (see page 96). Simple grills and sauceless dishes— grilled sausage or quail, for example—suggest the contrast of a creamy polenta made with a little more liquid (see Creamy Polenta Variation below).

At home, we often have a salad and plain polenta for dinner. Usually, I'll stir some grated Parmesan into the mixture when I add the butter. Or I'll pour the cooked polenta out onto a small wooden cutting board and put crumbled Gorgonzola or thin strips of Gruyère on top. I always look at that board and say I've made enough polenta for an army, but somehow we eat every bite.

4 cups water
¾ tsp. salt
1 cup polenta
3 Tb. unsalted butter

Bring water and salt to a boil in a heavy-bottomed saucepan. Add polenta in a slow, steady stream, whisking constantly with a wire whisk. Reduce heat to medium and cook, whisking constantly, about 3 minutes, or until mixture thickens perceptibly. Reduce heat to low and begin stirring with a wooden spoon. Cook, stirring almost constantly, until mixture is quite thick and no longer tastes grainy, 15 to 20 minutes. Remove from heat and stir in butter. Add more salt if desired.

Pour polenta onto a clean wooden or marble slab (such as a small cutting board) or, if you plan to cool it and slice it, pour it into a buttered sheet pan or cake pan. An 8-inch square cake pan will yield polenta about ¾-inch thick.

Polenta will harden as it cools.

Makes 4 servings.

BUYER'S NOTE

Fine-grained cornmeal of the sort used for American cornbread will not make an authentic polenta. Look for the coarse-grained meal, often identified as polenta, in Italian markets and health food stores.

CREAMY POLENTA VARIATION

Use 5 cups water to 1 cup polenta. To serve, spoon directly onto warm dinner plates.

Pan-Fried Polenta with Maple Syrup

The secret to good fried polenta is to cook it slowly in a cast-iron pan. And the best polenta for frying is polenta no more than about ⅓-inch thick. If your leftover polenta is thicker than that, slice it in half horizontally. Thin polenta gets crisp on both sides with just a smidgen of smoothness within. It's a sturdy, ski-cabin breakfast to have with stewed fruit and browned sausage.

Pour Basic Polenta into a buttered 9- by 13-inch pan and smooth the top. Let cool, then refrigerate several hours or overnight. Cut polenta into shapes as desired—triangles, diamonds or squares, for example—and set aside.

Basic Polenta (see page 92)
Unsalted butter
Pure maple syrup

Melt 2 tablespoons butter in each of two skillets, preferably cast-iron, over moderate heat. When butter sizzles and foams, divide polenta between the skillets and pan-fry slowly on both sides until golden brown and crusty, about 10 minutes total.

Transfer to warm serving plates, spread more butter on top and drizzle with warm maple syrup.

Makes 4 servings.

Red Pepper Polenta with Fontina

*I*n Italy, leftover polenta is the inspiration for countless dishes. Resourceful cooks slice it and layer it with meat sauce, mushroom sauce or good melting cheeses to make polenta torta(cake) or polenta pasticciata (a layered pie). In the version below, the polenta is flavored with oregano and sweet red pepper, then cooled, sliced and layered with creamy fontina. The assembled dish is baked until the cheese bubbles and browns on top. With a green salad and a fruit dessert, it's a dinner.*

6 Tb. unsalted butter
½ large onion, chopped
1 small red bell pepper, seeded, deribbed and minced
4 cups water
1 tsp. salt
1 cup polenta
2 Tb. minced parsley
1 tsp. minced fresh oregano
Freshly ground black pepper
½ pound Italian fontina cheese, grated
3 Tb. freshly grated Parmesan cheese
1 Tb. minced parsley, for garnish

Melt 3 tablespoons butter in a large skillet over moderate heat. Add onion and red pepper and sauté slowly until soft and sweet, about 20 minutes.

Meanwhile, bring water and salt to a boil in a heavy-bottomed 4-quart saucepan. Add polenta in a slow, steady stream, whisking constantly with a wire whisk. Reduce heat to low and begin stirring with a wooden spoon. Cook, stirring almost constantly, until mixture is quite thick and no longer tastes grainy, 15 to 20 minutes.

Stir softened onions and peppers, parsley and oregano into polenta. Stir in 2 tablespoons butter. Season to taste with pepper and more salt if necessary. Pour into a buttered 8-inch square baking pan and chill several hours until firm.

Preheat oven to 375°F.

Cut polenta into four squares and remove from pan with a spatula. Carefully cut each square horizontally in half. Arrange bottom halves in a buttered earthenware dish or return them to the 8-inch square baking pan. (It's nice to bake the polenta in an oven-to-table dish). Cover with two-thirds of the grated fontina. Top with the upper halves of polenta. Combine remaining fontina and the Parmesan and sprinkle over the top. Dot with remaining tablespoon butter. Bake until polenta is browned and bubbly, about 40 minutes. Let rest 5 minutes. Garnish with minced parsley before serving.

Makes 4 servings.

Polenta with Okra and Onions

Italians may not eat okra, but that shouldn't keep you from stirring it into a pot of creamy polenta. American southerners have been serving okra with cornbread for centuries. As a side dish, polenta with okra could partner grilled pork chops or spareribs; to make a one-dish meal, top it with strips of a melting cheese, like mozzarella or Italian fontina.

Trim ends of okra; cut okra into chunks about ⅓-inch wide. Melt 3 tablespoons butter in a large heavy skillet. Add onion and hot pepper flakes and sauté slowly until onion is soft, about 15 minutes. Add another tablespoon butter, okra and 3 tablespoons chicken stock. Cover and stew over low heat until okra is barely tender, about 15 minutes. Stir in garlic and cook 1 minute. Season with salt and pepper.

Bring 4 cups stock to a boil in a heavy-bottomed 4-quart saucepan. Add polenta in a slow, steady stream, whisking constantly. Reduce heat to medium and whisk until mixture thickens perceptibly. Reduce heat to low and begin stirring with a wooden spoon. Cook, stirring almost constantly, until mixture is quite thick and no longer tastes grainy, 15 to 20 minutes.

Stir okra/onion mixture gently into polenta. Taste and add more salt and pepper if necessary. Pour polenta out onto a marble or wooden slab. Dot the top with remaining tablespoon butter, cut into small bits. Serve immediately.

Makes 4 servings.

10 ounces okra
5 Tb. unsalted butter
2 cups chopped onion
Pinch hot red pepper flakes
4 cups plus 3 Tb. chicken stock (see COOK'S NOTE, page 14)
1 clove garlic, minced
Salt and freshly ground black pepper
1 cup polenta

VARIATION

Cut about 3 ounces of fresh mozzarella or Fontina into thin strips. Pour polenta out onto marble or wooden slab and lay the strips on top. Give them a moment to melt a little, then serve the polenta.

Polenta with Barolo Wine Sauce

A big, tannic Barolo will simmer down to a mellow sauce if flavored with vegetables and dried porcini and enriched with meaty veal bones. You can make the sauce a day ahead; in fact, it benefits from reheating, but don't swirl in the final butter addition until you reheat it.

1½ recipes Basic
  Polenta (see page 92)

SAUCE
1 ounce dried Italian
  porcini mushrooms
7 Tb. unsalted butter
2 carrots, diced
1 medium onion, diced
2 ribs celery, diced
½ pound mushrooms,
  sliced
3 cloves garlic, minced
1 tsp. minced fresh
  oregano
2 Tb. tomato paste
1 tsp. fennel seed
1 bay leaf
2 pounds meaty veal
  bones
1 750-ml. bottle Barolo
Salt and freshly ground
  black pepper

Spread cooked Polenta in a 13- by 9-inch baking dish and chill several hours until firm.

Meanwhile, cover *porcini* with 1 cup hot water and soak for 1 hour. Lift *porcini* out with a slotted spoon and rinse off any grit. Chop coarsely and set aside. Strain soaking liquid through a double thickness of cheesecloth and reserve.

Melt 4 tablespoons butter in a large stockpot over moderate heat. Add carrots, onion, celery and fresh mushrooms and sauté slowly, stirring occasionally, until softened, about 15 minutes. Stir in garlic, oregano, tomato paste, fennel seed, bay leaf, *porcini* and the strained soaking liquid. Stew gently 5 minutes.

Preheat oven to 450°F. Put veal bones in a lightly oiled baking dish and roast until well-browned and crusty, about 30 minutes. Transfer the veal bones to the stockpot; deglaze baking dish with ½ cup Barolo, scraping up any browned bits clinging to the bottom of the dish. Add to the stockpot along with the remaining wine.

Cover pot and simmer on lowest heat for about 3 hours. Check occasionally to make sure it is not cooking too fast or reducing too much. Move the pot halfway off the burner if necessary and add ¼ cup of water if sauce is too thick. Uncover pot during final half-hour if sauce is not thick enough. After about 3 hours, the sauce will be a rich, deep brown and the wine flavor will have mellowed. Remove and discard veal bones and bay leaf. Season sauce to taste with salt and pepper.

Cut polenta into desired shapes and arrange on a buttered sheet pan or in a buttered baking dish. Bake in a preheated 350°F. oven until hot throughout, about 20 minutes. Divide hot polenta among six warm serving plates; swirl remaining 3 tablespoons butter into sauce, then spoon sauce over polenta.

Makes 6 servings.

Polenta with Hickory-Smoked Spareribs

The hickory flavor really comes through in these meaty smoked ribs because there's no sticky sweet barbecue sauce to cover it up. The ribs marinate for a day in wine, rosemary, fennel and a little tomato paste to give the smoke some sugar to work on. Don't overcook these ribs. After 20 to 25 minutes, they should be tender and juicy.

Combine wine, tomato paste, garlic, onion, fennel seed, rosemary, oil and several grinds of black pepper in a saucepan. Bring to a boil, reduce heat to low, cover and simmer 20 minutes. Cool.

Put spareribs in a glass, enamel or stainless steel dish. Cover with cooled wine marinade. Cover dish with plastic wrap and marinate in the refrigerator for 24 hours, turning several times. Bring ribs to room temperature before grilling.

Prepare a medium-hot charcoal fire. When the coals are gray, arrange them in a ring around the perimeter of the grill. Nestle an aluminum foil drip pan in the middle. Lift hickory chips out of their water and put them in the drip pan.

Salt spareribs on both sides, then arrange them on the grill, positioning them over the drip pan. Brush ribs with some of the marinade. Cover and smoke 10 to 12 minutes. Uncover, turn and brush with marinade, then cover and smoke an additional 10 to 12 minutes.

Meanwhile, cook polenta.

Let spareribs rest 5 minutes before carving into ribs. To serve, divide hot polenta and ribs among four warm plates.

Makes 4 servings.

3 cups dry red or white wine
3 Tb. tomato paste
6 cloves garlic, peeled and smashed
1 large onion, sliced
2 tsp. fennel seed
3 sprigs fresh rosemary
¾ cup olive oil
Freshly ground black pepper
3 pounds meaty spareribs
2 cups hickory chips, soaked in water to cover for 1 hour
Coarse salt
Basic Polenta (see page 92)

Polenta with Pan-Fried Quail

Wild quail may require some moist cooking in a slow oven, but the farm-raised quail in the markets are tender enough for quick cooking. Stuff thyme and garlic in their cavities for flavor, then brown them well in fresh bacon fat. The plump browned birds can then be "nested" on a platter of Creamy Polenta and served family-style. On another occasion, consider serving the pan-fried quail with wild rice.

6 fresh quail, head and feet removed

Salt and freshly ground black pepper

6 sprigs fresh thyme

6 garlic cloves, peeled and halved

6 slices bacon

1 Tb. unsalted butter

Basic Polenta—
Creamy Variation
(see page 92)

2 Tb. minced parsley

Rinse quail, dry thoroughly and generously salt and pepper inside and out. Stuff each cavity with a sprig of fresh thyme and a halved garlic clove.

Render bacon slowly in a large skillet, preferably cast-iron. Remove bacon strips when crisp and keep warm in a low oven. Pour off all but 3 tablespoons bacon fat. Add butter to pan, raise heat to medium-high and add quail. Brown quail well all over, beginning with one side, then the other, then the back, then the breast, about 10 minutes total.

Pour polenta onto a large warm serving platter with a rim. Top with pan-fried quail and arrange bacon strips between the quail. Garnish with minced parsley.

Makes 3 servings.

Polenta Country Cake
with Fresh Peaches

This simple cake is so soft and moist it's almost a custard or pudding. But when barely warm, it can be sliced into neat wedges and eaten with a fork. Serve it with coffee or a glass of sweet wine. Fresh figs in summer or pears in winter can substitute for the peaches.

Bring milk to a simmer in a heavy saucepan over moderate heat. Add polenta in a slow steady stream, whisking constantly. When mixture returns to a simmer, reduce heat to low and cook, whisking constantly, until mixture thickens perceptibly. Add ¼ cup sugar and pinch salt and stir with a wooden spoon. Continue stirring until mixture is smooth and thick, about 15 minutes. Stir in butter and remove from heat. Cool 2 minutes, then stir in vanilla and eggs. Mix well to blend.

Preheat oven to 375°F.

Pour batter into a buttered 8-inch round cake pan. Arrange peach wedges neatly on top. Sprinkle with remaining tablespoon sugar. Bake in the preheated oven until firm to the touch and lightly browned, 40 to 45 minutes. Cool on a rack. Serve warm with whipped cream.

Makes 8 servings.

1½ cups milk
½ cup polenta
¼ cup plus 1 Tb. sugar
Pinch salt
2 Tb. unsalted butter
¼ tsp. pure vanilla extract
3 eggs, lightly beaten
1 peach, peeled, cut into 12 wedges and sprinkled with lemon juice
Lightly sweetened whipped cream

Polentina

The Piedmontese of northern Italy turn polenta into a creamy pudding by simmering it with milk, eggs, sugar and lemon peel. Like rice pudding, Polentina is a homespun dessert. Save it for simple kitchen dinners when you don't mind standing and stirring at the stove with guests around.

½ cup golden raisins
¼ cup sweet white wine
  or water
4 cups milk
½ tsp. salt
4 eggs, lightly beaten
6 Tb. sugar
2 strips lemon peel
½ cup plus 2 Tb.
  polenta
Heavy cream, optional

Plump raisins in wine or water overnight. Whisk together milk, salt, eggs, sugar and lemon peel in a heavy saucepan. Bring to a simmer over medium-high heat, whisking constantly. Add polenta in a slow, steady stream and cook, whisking constantly, until mixture thickens. Reduce heat to low and cook, whisking often, until polenta loses its gritty texture and becomes creamy, about 15 minutes. Stir in raisins and the soaking liquid. Remove lemon peel. Serve in warm bowls or goblets, with a pitcher of cold heavy cream.

Makes 6 generous servings, about 4½ cups total.

Wild Rice

Wild Rice

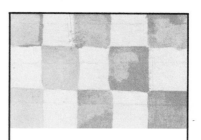

What we call wild rice is actually not rice at all but the seed of a grass native to Minnesota. It grows abundantly there in lakes, rivers and lowlands and was a staple in the Native American diet as early as the 1600s.

In Minnesota's natural wild rice stands, Native Americans still harvest by the traditional "canoe and flail" method: one person stands in the canoe, poling it through the stand, while the other maneuvers two sticks, a three-foot-long one to bend the stalk into the canoe and a much shorter one to thrash out the seed. What falls into the water instead of the canoe and what shatters off the stalk before harvest become next year's crop.

Wild rice is an increasingly important crop in California, where it is seeded by air and harvested by machine. The quality is excellent and the price is half to two-thirds that of Minnesota rice.

Wild rice has an earthy flavor that is particularly appealing with game and rich meats. The grain can be ground into flour and used, in combination with white flour, for pancakes, waffles, crepes, muffins and other baked goods. Mix the grain with white rice or brown rice for pilafs or cold salads; stir it into soups or use it as the foundation for a poultry stuffing.

A CHAMPAGNE BREAKFAST

The following menu appeals to me for a winter brunch, a New Year's Day breakfast or a midnight supper. The main course would be delicious with Champagne.

Endive, Watercress and Avocado Salad

Creamed Turkey and Giblets

Wild Rice Waffles (page 110)

Prune, Pear and Quince Compote

Basic Wild Rice

*O*ne of my husband's former business partners was a wild rice grower. He and his family ate wild rice as casually and often as we eat potatoes.

One autumn shortly after the rice harvest, we drove up to his paddies to glean some of the grain the mechanical harvesters missed. "Take as much as you like," Dick said, with a twinkle in his eye.

We helped ourselves, but as we quickly discovered, harvesting is the easy part. Lacking a neighborhood processing plant, we had to separate the seed from the husk the old-fashioned way. I had a magazine article that described the traditional method the native Americans used, so we set to work.

First, we spread the grain out on mats to ferment in the sun for a couple of days. Then we toasted it slowly in a skillet (in theory, over an open fire) to give it a smoky flavor and to loosen the husk. Then we took it back outside, put on soft-soled shoes (in theory, moccasins) and stomped on it to separate the seed from the husk. At least that's the way the native Americans do it.

Even before we got to the fourth and final step of tossing the grains back and forth in baskets to let the breeze blow away the chaff, it was clear that our seeds were still firmly ensconced in their husks. And it was beginning to be clear why Minnesota wild rice is so expensive. Humbled, we packed up our treading shoes and threw out the grain. Today we buy our wild rice fully processed and are grateful for it.

1 cup wild rice
Water
Salt, to taste
Butter

Put wild rice in a sieve and rinse well under cold running water. Let drain. Bring 3 inches of lightly salted water to a boil in a medium saucepan. Add rice, stir once with a fork, and boil, uncovered, over high heat until rice tastes barely tender, about 35 minutes. Drain rice well in colander; discard cooking liquid or save for soup.

Put an inch of water in a large saucepan and bring to a boil. Put rice in a large sieve or steamer and set over the boiling water; cover rice with a damp folded tea towel and the lid. Steam 15 minutes. Uncover, remove tea towel and transfer rice to a warm serving dish. Add salt and butter to taste and fluff with a fork.

Makes 4 servings, 3 cups total.

BUYER'S NOTE

Many supermarkets carry packaged wild rice; some also offer it in bulk. Natural-food stores and specialty shops are another good source for wild rice. Although Californians and Minnesotans may debate the relative merits of their state's wild rice, it is difficult to find consistent differences between them. How the rice is processed is more important than where it is grown. Look for long uniform grains; avoid bulk wild rice with a lot of broken grains.

Wild Rice with Wild Mushroom Butter

Dried Italian porcini *mushrooms* (boletus edulis) *add an intense, woodsy flavor to rice and pasta, soups and stews. They're expensive but you don't need much to impart a rich fragrance to a dish. "Cut" them with fresh supermarket button mushrooms, then braise them in butter with minced shallots and stir them into wild rice. Serve the rice with turkey, duck, quail, squab or wild game. For a less expensive version, substitute barley for wild rice.*

Cover *porcini* with 1 cup hot water and soak for 1 hour. Lift *porcini* out with a slotted spoon and rinse off any grit. Chop fine. Strain soaking liquid through a double thickness of cheesecloth and set aside.

Melt 2 tablespoons butter in a large skillet over moderate heat. Add shallots and sauté briefly until softened. Add porcini and button mushrooms; sauté until softened, about 5 minutes. Add 3 tablespoons porcini soaking liquid and simmer until thoroughly absorbed. Season mushrooms with salt and pepper and remove from heat. (Save remaining porcini soaking liquid for soups or stews.)

Cook wild rice and transfer it to a warm serving bowl. Add sautéed mushrooms and remaining 1½ tablespoons butter, stirring them in with two forks. Season to taste with salt and pepper.

Makes 4 servings.

¾ ounce dried *porcini* mushrooms
3½ Tb. unsalted butter
2 Tb. minced shallots
1 cup finely minced button mushrooms
Salt and freshly ground black pepper
Basic Wild Rice (see page 104)

Wild Rice with Bacon, Scallions and Peas

*T*his dish is far more delicious than its few ingredients and quick preparation would suggest. It's most easily made in a wok, but a large skillet will do if you treat the grains carefully as you stir-fry them. This Westernized fried rice would be good with turkey, duck or quail; any leftovers can be stirred into chicken broth the next day.

5 slices bacon, cut into ¼-inch widths

6 scallions, white and light green part only, thinly sliced

1 cup cooked peas

Basic Wild Rice, cooled (see page 104)

Salt and freshly ground black pepper

Render bacon bits until crisp; transfer to paper towels to drain. Pour off all but 2 tablespoons bacon fat in skillet. Add scallions and cook over moderately high heat until slightly softened, about 2 minutes. Add peas and stir to coat with bacon fat. Add cooked rice and cook, stirring or tossing with a flat spatula, until rice is hot throughout. Stir in bacon. Season to taste with salt and pepper. Transfer to a warm serving bowl and serve immediately.

Makes 4 to 6 servings.

Four-Grain Pilaf

Mixing grains is a good way to stretch the more expensive wild rice. Besides, in many cases the grains are more appealing in combination. The soft texture of barley juxtaposed with chewy wild rice, the dusty color of brown rice against the dark wild rice are appetizing contrasts that make dishes better than the sum of their parts.

The pilaf below isn't made by traditional pilaf methods. Instead, the grains are steamed and cooled, then stir-fried with butter-stewed onions and peppers just before serving. Serve the dish with grilled chops—veal, lamb or pork; with peppery roast duck or chicken; or with braised quail.

⅓ cup whole oats
⅓ cup wild rice
⅓ cup barley
⅓ cup brown rice
2 Tb. unsalted butter
1 cup chopped onion
⅔ cup minced red bell pepper
Salt and freshly ground black pepper

Bring 2½ cups lightly salted water to a boil in a large saucepan. Add oats, cover, reduce heat and simmer for 15 minutes. Add wild rice, barley and brown rice; stir once with a fork, cover and cook over low heat for 40 minutes. Transfer cooked grains to a sieve and let any extra liquid drain off, then spread grains out on a tray or in a baking dish and let cool at least 10 minutes. (Grains may be cooked several hours ahead; let them cool, then cover the dish with plastic wrap and leave at room temperature.)

Melt butter in a wok or a large skillet over moderately low heat. Add onion and bell pepper and sauté, stirring often, until softened, about 10 minutes. Raise heat to medium-high. Add grains and cook, carefully tossing with a flat spatula, until they are hot throughout. Season to taste with salt and pepper. Serve immediately.

Makes 6 servings, about 4½ cups total.

Wild Rice, Watercress and Pecan Stuffing

*T*uck *this simple stuffing inside any kind of poultry or into the cavity of a whole fresh salmon. If you can find arugula (also known as rocket or roquette), substitute it for watercress. It adds a lovely nutty flavor to the stuffing. Allow ¾ cup stuffing per pound of uncooked poultry, and stuff your bird only shortly before roasting.*

½ cup raisins

2 Tb. bourbon

3½ cups chicken stock or water (see COOK'S NOTE, page 14)

1 cup wild rice

1 cup barley

2 cups pecan halves

3 Tb. unsalted butter

2 bunches scallions, white and light green parts only, sliced

2½ cups coarsely chopped watercress

Salt and freshly ground black pepper

Plump raisins in ¼ cup very warm water mixed with bourbon for one hour. Drain well.

Bring 2 cups chicken stock or salted water to a boil; add wild rice, cover and cook over low heat for 40 minutes.

Meanwhile, bring 1½ cups chicken stock or salted water to a boil in another saucepan; add barley, cover and cook over low heat for 30 minutes or until barely done.

Toast pecans on a baking sheet in a preheated 325°F. oven until fragrant, about 10 minutes. Let cool, then chop coarsely. Melt butter in a skillet over moderate heat. Add scallions and sauté until softened. In a large bowl, combine scallions, cooked rice, cooked barley, nuts, watercress and drained raisins. Stir with a fork to blend, then season to taste with salt and pepper.

Makes about 10 cups, enough for a 14-pound turkey.